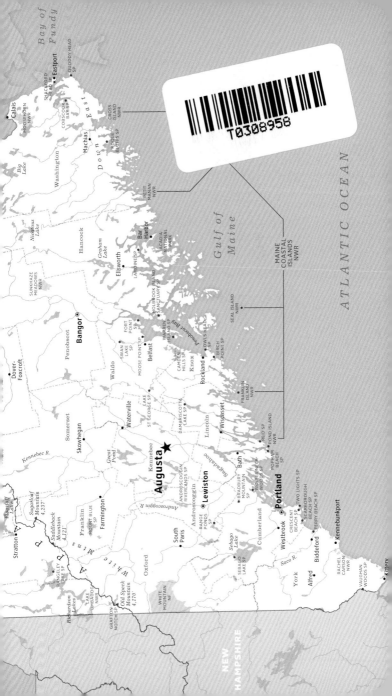

American Birding Association

Field Guide to Birds of Maine

Nick Lund

PHOTOGRAPHS BY
Brian E. Small
AND OTHERS

Scott & Nix, Inc.
NEW YORK

A SCOTT & NIX EDITION

PUBLISHED BY SCOTT & NIX, INC.
150 W 28TH ST, STE 1900
NEW YORK, NY 10001
SCOTTANDNIX.COM

FIRST EDITION 2022

ISBN 978-1-935622-74-1

AMERICAN BIRDING ASSOCIATION, INC.
800-850-2473
ABA.ORG

SCOTT & NIX, INC. BOOKS
ARE DISTRIBUTED TO THE TRADE BY

INDEPENDENT PUBLISHERS GROUP (IPG)
814 NORTH FRANKLIN STREET
CHICAGO, IL 60610
800-888-4741
IPGBOOK.COM

THIS BOOK IS PRINTED ON FSC® CERTIFIED PAPERS,
WHICH ASSURES IT WAS MADE FROM WELL MANAGED
FORESTS AND OTHER CONTROLLED SOURCES.

PRINTED IN THE REPUBLIC OF KOREA

Contents

vii *American Birding Association Mission Statement* AND *Code of Ethics*

xi *Foreword*
BY JEFFREY A. GORDON, PRESIDENT, AMERICAN BIRDING ASSOCIATION

xiii *Introduction*
BIRDS IN MAINE *xiii*
BECOMING A BIRDER *xvii*
A YEAR IN MAINE BIRDING *xx*
BIRDS IN THS GUIDE *xxv*
PARTS OF A BIRD *xxvii*
RESOURCES *xxx*

2 Geese

4 Ducks

35 Grouse

37 Turkey

38 Loons

41 Grebes

44 Petrels

46 Shearwaters

50 Fulmar

51 Gannet

52 Cormorants

55 Wading Birds

64 Osprey

66 Vulture

68 Hawks

79 Falcons

84 Owls

90 Rails

92 Gallinule

93 Coot

94 Crane

96 Shorebirds

126 Gulls

137 Terns

142 Jaeger

143 Alcids

150 Pigeon

151 Dove

152 Cuckoos

154 Nightjars

156 Swift

157 Kingfisher

158 Hummingbird

160 Woodpeckers

168 Flycatchers

177 Shrike

178 Vireos

183 Lark

184 Jays

186 Raven

188 Crows

190 Swallows

196 Chickadees

199 Titmouse

200 Nuthatches

202 Creeper

203 Wrens

207 Gnatcatcher

208 Kinglets

210 Thrushes

218 Catbird

219 Thrasher

220 Mockingbird

221 Pipit

222 Starling

223 House Sparrow

224 Waxwings

226 Longspur

227 Bunting

228 Warblers

257 Towhee

258 Sparrows

274 Tanager

275 Cardinal

276 Grosbeak

277 Bunting

278 Blackbirds

284 Orioles

287 Finches

296 *Acknowledgments*

297 *Image Credits*

298 *Maine Bird Records Committee Checklist of Maine Birds*

303 *Species Index*

The American Birding Association inspires all people to enjoy and protect wild birds.

The ABA represents the North American birding community and supports birders through publications, conferences, workshops, events, partnerships, and networks.

The ABA's education programs promote birding skills, ornithological knowledge, and the development of and implementation of a conservation ethic.

The ABA encourages birders to apply their skills to help conserve birds and their habitats, and we represent the interests of birders in planning and legislative arenas.

We welcome all birders as members.

THE AMERICAN BIRDING ASSOCIATION CODE OF ETHICS

1. **Respect and promote birds and their environment.**

   (a) Support the conservation of birds and their habitats. Engage in and promote bird-friendly practices whenever possible, such as keeping cats and other domestic animals indoors or controlled, acting to prevent window strikes, maintaining safe feeding stations, landscaping with native plants, drinking shade-grown coffee, and advocating for conservation policies. Be mindful of any negative environmental impacts of your activities, including contributing to climate change. Reduce or offset such impacts as much as you are able.

   (b) Avoid stressing birds or exposing them to danger. Be particularly cautious around active nests and nesting colonies, roosts, display sites, and feeding sites. Limit the use of recordings and other audio methods of attracting birds, particularly in heavily birded areas, for species that are rare in the area, and for species that are threatened or endangered. Always exercise caution and restraint when photographing, recording, or otherwise approaching birds.

(c) Always minimize habitat disturbance. Consider the benefits of staying on trails, preserving snags, and similar practices.

2. **Respect and promote the birding community and its individual members.**

(a) Be an exemplary ethical role model by following this Code and leading by example. Always bird and report with honesty and integrity.

(b) Respect the interests, rights, and skill levels of fellow birders, as well as people participating in other outdoor activities. Freely share your knowledge and experience and be especially helpful to beginning birders.

(c) Share bird observations freely, provided such reporting would not violate other sections of this Code, as birders, ornithologists, and conservationists derive considerable benefit from publicly available bird sightings.

(d) Approach instances of perceived unethical birding behavior with sensitivity and respect; try to resolve the matter in a positive manner, keeping in mind that perspectives vary. Use the situation as an opportunity to teach by example and to introduce more people to this Code.

(e) In group birding situations, promote knowledge by everyone in the group of the practices in this Code and ensure that the group does not unduly interfere with others using the same area.

3. **Respect and promote the law and the rights of others.**

(a) Never enter private property without the landowner's permission. Respect the interests of and interact positively with people living in the area where you are birding.

(b) Familiarize yourself with and follow all laws, rules, and regulations governing activities at your birding location. In particular, be aware of regulations related to birds, such as disturbance of protected nesting areas or sensitive habitats, and the use of audio or food lures. Everyone who enjoys birds and birding must always respect wildlife, its environment, and the rights of others. In any conflict of interest between birds and birders, the welfare of the birds and their environment comes first.

Birding should be fun and help build a better future for birds, for birders, and for all people

Birds and birding opportunities are shared resources that should be open and accessible to all

Birders should always give back more than they take

Foreword

If you call Maine home or just visit from time to time, you know of its many charms. What you may not yet realize is just how good the Pine Tree State is for birding. This book will open your eyes to a world of discoveries starting right at your doorstep. From the teeming coastal waters Downeast to the forest of the Allagash, there is a wealth of bird life to enjoy here all year long.

Like all the guides in this series, this book can help you do whatever you want with birding. Perhaps you enjoy birds a few days a year in your yard or local park and just want to know a little more about them and to know some of their names. Or maybe you want to dive deeper and really get familiar with the hundreds of amazing birds that call Maine home for part or all of each year. Our aim is to meet you where you are and give you useful, reliable information and insight into birds and birding.

Nick Lund, who is outreach and network manager for Maine Audubon and runs The Birdist blog, is a life-long birder and the perfect guide for those wanting to explore the birds of Maine. You're in very good hands with him. The gorgeous photography by Brian Small and others will not only aid your identifica-tions—it will inspire you to get out and see more of these beautiful and fascinating creatures for yourself.

I invite you to visit the American Birding Association website (aba.org), where you'll find a wealth of free resources and ways to connect with the birding community that will also help you get the most from your birding in Maine and beyond. Please consider becoming an ABA member yourself—one of the best parts of birding is joining a community of fun, passionate people.

Now get on out there! Enjoy this book. Enjoy Maine. And most of all, enjoy birding!

Good birding,

Jeffrey A. Gordon

Jeffrey A. Gordon, *President*
American Birding Association

Birds in Maine

Maine left Massachusetts in 1820 to become its own state and took the best of New England with it.

When all of the sandy beaches, rocky inlets, and wave-splashed islands are counted, Maine's jagged shoreline is longer than California's. The northern reaches of the Appalachian Mountains bisect the state from the west, forming tumbling rivers that drain into a broad gulf hosting some of the most famous fishing grounds in the world. And, everywhere, forests: Maine is the most forested state in the nation, from the broad-leaved deciduous and mixed forests in the south to deep, dark, boreal spruce-fir stretches in the north and far east. In each of these habitats and others, there are birds.

In a 1927 proposal to establish a state bird for Maine, the State Federation of Women's Clubs wrote that chickadees expressed the "qualities of optimism, cheeriness, friendliness, resourcefulness, and industry," which "stand forth as qualities of the citizens of Maine."

Of course, Maine's landscape long predates statehood. Twenty-
one thousand years ago, the land that became Maine was
beneath the immense Laurentide Ice Sheet. Climatic warming
was pushing the glaciers north, scouring the land as they went.
The coast was exposed some 16,000–17,000 years ago, and the
last of the ice left what is now northern Maine about 13,000
years ago. Vegetation crept onto the exposed earth, and in the
first few thousand years after the ice receded, much of Maine
was covered in tundra, similar to Labrador today. Humans
arrived at least 12,000 years ago, and by the time of European
colonization in the 1600s, an estimated 25,000 Native Americans—the Maliseet, Micmac, Penobscot, and Passamaquoddy,
known collectively as the Wabanaki, or "People of the Dawn-
land"—were in what is now Maine.

The arrival of Europeans hastened the pace of a changing
landscape. The first sawmill was built in South Berwick in
1634, just 30 years after the first Europeans settled on St. Croix
Island in the upper reaches of Passamaquoddy Bay and at
Popham Colony, at what is now Popham Beach. Lumber sourced
from the vast forests of the interior and fish caught in the Gulf
of Maine drove Maine's economy for centuries. The state's
growing population cleared woodlands to support agriculture,
a phenomenon that peaked around 1880, when about 30 percent
of the entire state was in farmland.

Despite its thriving industries, Maine held fast to a reputation
for rugged wilderness. Remote sporting camps thrived in the
1800s, taking advantage of abundant fish and game. Henry
David Thoreau collected separate journeys in the 1840s and
1850s into The Maine Woods, published posthumously in 1864,
and helped solidify the public image of Maine as one of
uninterrupted nature. The state has been home or an inspiration to famous sportsmen and women, naturalists, and
conservationists, including John James Audubon, Theodore
Roosevelt, Cornelia Thurza "Fly Rod" Crosby, Rachel Carson, Ed
Muskie, and many more. The state's abundant nature and
wilderness character remain an inspiration to Mainers and
Maine lovers around the nation.

Greatly simplified, Maine's geography can be divided into three separate zones: the eastern forests of southern and central Maine; the boreal forests of the western mountains, north, and northeast, aka Downeast Maine; and the coast and offshore islands. The eastern forest zone of northern hardwoods, agricultural lands, and developed areas covers the general area from Kittery in the south to about halfway up the New Hampshire border, and inland to the Bangor area. These oak, pine, and mixed-species hardwood forests provide habitat for a large mix of bird species, some of which—including the Red-bellied Woodpecker, Orchard Oriole, and Glossy Ibis—reach the northern limit of their breeding range.

Roughly halfway up the state, Maine's forests transition from eastern hardwoods to boreal forests. The dense spruce-fir forests that begin along the northern half of the New Hampshire border to the west run up through the mountains past Baxter State Park to the northern border with Canada and down to Downeast Maine. They are home to certain species

The Purple Sandpiper is one of the hardy few shorebirds tolerant of a Maine winter.

never or rarely found anywhere south, including the Spruce
Grouse, Boreal Chickadee, and Canada Jay, and provide
nurseries for millions of migratory warblers, vireos, flycatchers,
and other species. Maine's boreal forests are considered part of
North America's "baby bird factory," the southern edge of a
massive and critically important biome covering much of
Canada and Alaska.

Offshore, the rocky islands and fish-filled Gulf of Maine
provide food for dozens of nesting seabirds, including the
species that might be Maine's most iconic: the Atlantic Puffin.
Maine is the only state with a breeding population of Atlantic
Puffins, restored in the 1970s through an ongoing effort by
the National Audubon Society. The more than 73 offshore
islands comprising the Maine Coastal Islands National Wildlife
Refuge provide habitat for puffins, as well as terns, guillemots,
Razorbills, Common Eiders, murres, and other species that
breed in few other American locations. These habitats, along
with scattered wetlands, beaches, krummholz, grassland, and
open ocean, make Maine one of the nation's most exciting states
for birders.

In the summer months,
birders can schedule a
boat tour to see
Maine's iconic Atlantic
Puffins on breeding
colonies offshore.

Becoming a Birder

Whenever someone asks me what's so great about birding, I think about rock climbing. I know and respect rock climbers and, let's be honest, am jealous of their strength and agility, but I can only imagine it's a frustrating passion. How difficult it must be to be stuck at work when all you want to do is go rock climbing! How disappointing, when you finally have time to get to the wall, and it's raining, or too windy, or too hot or cold! How bittersweet to travel to visit family in some non-climbable area, only to have the mind constantly occupied with thoughts of faraway rocks!

Birders have none of these problems. Birders can always bird: At work, through an office window, during a lunch break. In the rain and wind and snow and ice and heat, in cities or towns, along coasts, on mountains, or at a highway rest stop, at night or during the day. There is no such thing as "traveling away from birds," only new species to find in new locations. The beauty of birding is that it is so considerate, so giving, that it is available anytime, anywhere.

Importantly, "anytime" means not just at any time of the year but also at any age. Birding, quite rare among outdoor hobbies and certainly a major point of separation from rock climbing, has no age cap. People can become birders at a young age and remain birders for as long as they've got a window to look out or ears to hear the dawn chorus. You can be a birder any day or all the days of your life.

The endless availability of birding means that many approaches are possible, and there are many kinds of birders. Some birders pursue the hobby with a passion. Ask these birders why they bird, and the answer you get may be "to see all the birds," and to accomplish that goal, passionate birders travel all over the state, country, or globe, keeping lists, chasing rarities, waking up at ungodly hours, and otherwise exuding an obsession with birds. These people are sometimes derided as "listers," but the epithet rarely fazes them: the bird-obsessed are having the time of their lives. Their kind of adventurous, all-encompassing birding is a joyful life filled with outdoor exploration, spontaneity, and an endless fascination with nature.

Keeping track of what they've seen is a big part of birding for these people, and for many other kinds of birders. The bird-obsessed often maintain all sorts of lists: of birds seen in their yard, or of birds seen throughout the state, or in particular counties, or months, or anything. Comparing these lists, and wanting to have the "biggest" list for a particular division, is where a competitive spirit arises that some birders find off-putting, but it is not an important aspect of the hobby: the birders with the biggest list aren't considered the "best" birders; they're just the ones who've had the time and opportunity (and money) to track everything down.

For the intrigued, the Big Year record for Maine (most species seen in a calendar year) is currently held by Josh Fecteau, who saw 317 species in Maine in 2017. Maine's Big Day record (most species seen in a single day from midnight to midnight) is a whopping 187 species seen by Bill Sheehan, Lysle Brinker, Robby Lambert, and David Ladd on May 30, 2011. Altogether,

Wild Turkey. Extirpated from the state around the turn of the 20th century, Wild Turkeys have made a dramatic recovery due in large part to the creation of hunting regulations.

461 different bird species have ever been found in Maine, but only a very few dedicated birders ever reach the 400 mark. Godspeed, if this is how you enjoy birding.

The vast majority of birders pursue their hobby more casually. A 2011 survey by the U.S. Fish and Wildlife Service found that more than 41 million Americans across the country self-identify as "around-the-home" birders, while 18 million claim they are more active "away-from-home" birders. Birding from home can mean setting up bird feeders in the backyard and noticing what visits; it can mean working on taking excellent photographs; it can mean following along as eggs hatch in a nest in the eaves; and it can mean just trying to figure out what that bird was you saw that one time. There aren't many "around-the-home" rock climbers, but birding is a hobby big enough to welcome anyone with an interest in birds, in any way they want. Welcome.

The Mourning Warbler breeds in regenerating areas of the boreal forest.

A Year in Maine Birding

The rich variety of Maine's ecosystems provides year-round birding opportunities. One of birding's true joys is looking forward to something new with each turn of the season. Pity the skiers hanging up their poles in April, or kayakers putting their boats under a tarp for the winter! For birders, each month brings a new adventure—if you know where to look.

JANUARY. The height of winter holds surprises for the dedicated birder. Sea watching at winter headlands may produce sought-after alcids, such as the Razorbill, Thick-billed Murre, or Dovekie, or rafts of sea ducks, including scoters, the Harlequin Duck, Common Eider, and Red-breasted Merganser. Arriving early is a good bet to catch alcids in flight on their way to feeding grounds. Sea Watch Hotspots: Nubble Point in York, East Point Audubon Sanctuary at Biddeford Pool, Dyer Point and Two Lights State Park in Cape Elizabeth, Pemaquid Point, and Schoodic Peninsula.

FEBRUARY. A keen birder will notice the earliest signs of spring migration, including the return of Red-winged Blackbirds and Common Grackles. Great Horned Owls are among the earliest nesting birds. For some birders, February excitement

Blue-winged Teal. These ducks are present as breeders in northern Maine and seen elsewhere during spring and fall migration.

can be found in the chance of finding rare gulls wintering in Maine. Best to look wherever gulls congregate, including wharves, fish hatcheries, landfills, and beaches. Winter Gull Hotspots: Portland Harbor, the Bangor waterfront, Owls Head Harbor, the Bath riverfront, and Dyer Point in Cape Elizabeth.

MARCH. Spring migration begins in earnest, as large numbers of waterfowl, as well as Ospreys, Eastern Phoebes, Great Blue Herons, and other species, begin to move up into ice-free lakes and ponds. Waterfowl Migration Hotspots: Scarborough Marsh, Sanford Lagoons, Wharton Point in Brunswick, Cobbosseecontee Lake in Manchester, Sabattus Pond, Weskeag Marsh, Penjajawoc Marsh in Bangor, and more.

APRIL. Migration heats up as many new species return to a greening state. They include the earliest of the warblers, hawks and other raptors, shorebirds, and swallows. Many migrants arrive in southern Maine a week or so before arriving in the Bangor area, and in Bangor itself perhaps a week ahead of parts farther north. Southern Maine Migration Hotspots: Evergreen Cemetery in Portland, Kennebunk Plains, Biddeford Pool, River Point Conservation Area in Falmouth, Fort Foster in Kittery, Bradbury Mountain State Park, and many more.

Blackburnian Warbler. The fire-throated Blackburnian Warbler is one of more than 20 species of warbler that breeds regularly in Maine.

MAY. This is the month that birders dream about, as colorful migrants seem to perch on every branch and bird song fills the air. There is no bad birding in May. Central and Midcoast Maine Migration Hotspots: Essex Woods, Taylor Bait Farm, Penjajawoc Marsh, and Orono Bog Walk in Bangor; Viles Arboretum in Augusta; Sears Island in Searsport; Unity Pond; Merryspring Nature Park in Camden; and many others.

JUNE. Peak nesting season throughout the state is a great time of year to observe mating displays, nest building, singing, territorial defense, and other behaviors. It's also when Atlantic Puffins and other seabirds may be seen at Maine's famous offshore nesting islands. Offshore Seabird Hotspots (visitation options vary): Matinicus Rock, Eastern Egg Rock, Isle of Shoals, Machias Seal Island, and Petit Manan, plus offshore ferries and whale-watching trips from Portland, Bar Harbor, Boothbay Harbor, and elsewhere.

JULY. The woods quiet down as birds feed and care for their young. July is a great time to visit the woods of northern Maine, part of North America's "baby bird factory," to witness its incredible productivity. Boreal Birding Hotspots: the Rangeley area, the Carrabassett Valley area, Old Speck Mountain, Baxter State Park and Katahdin Woods and Waters National Monu-

These songbirds can be impressively common at coastal hotspots during fall migration.

ment, the Topsfield area, Boot Head Preserve in Lubec, Roque Bluffs State Park, and Aroostook NWR.

AUGUST. Shorebirds return south from Arctic breeding grounds, kicking off peak shorebird season in Maine. Flocks of flighty little shorebirds pose identification challenges for many birders but reward the patient, the studious, and the lucky. Shorebird Hotspots: Lubec Flats, Popham Beach, Reid State Park, Pine Point in Scarborough, Biddeford Pool and Hills Beach, Crescent Beach in Scarborough, and more.

SEPTEMBER. Considering newly fledged birds, fall migration involves more individual birds than spring migration, though plumages are often muted and the birds are quieter. Most hotspots are similar to those in spring, though there are some favored fall locations. Fall Migration Hotspots: Monhegan Island, Sandy Point Beach on Cousins Island in Yarmouth, Quoddy Head State Park, Acadia National Park, Laudholm Farm, and more.

OCTOBER. Generally, warblers and other insect-eating birds move south in September, while seed-eating birds, such as sparrows, move later to take advantage of maturing seeds and ripe berries. Grasslands or meadow habitats are great places to

Northern Saw-whet Owl. This diminutive owl is likely the most common owl species in Maine, though spotting it can be difficult.

find sparrows in all seasons, but grasslands are disappearing in the state. Grassland Hotspots: Kennebunk Plains, Great Salt Bay Farm Wildlife Preserve in Damariscotta, Brunswick Landing, West Penjajawoc Grasslands in Bangor, California Fields Wildlife Area in Hollis, blueberry barrens Downeast, and agricultural fields in Aroostook County.

NOVEMBER. New birds arrive in Maine: species that spend their summers farther north and come to ride out the comparatively mild Maine winters. These include waterfowl such as the Bufflehead and Common Goldeneye and nomadic finches such as the Pine Grosbeak and Common Redpoll. Winter birding can be a challenge but rewards the dedicated and the adventurous. Winter Birding Hotspots: Biddeford Pool, Dyer Point and Two Lights State Park in Cape Elizabeth, Passamaquoddy Bay, Schoodic Peninsula, Marginal Way in Ogunquit, Sabattus Pond, Scarborough Marsh, and more.

DECEMBER. This is the month for the Christmas Bird Count, the famous census of birdlife that the National Audubon Society (audubon.org) has organized for more than 120 years running. Birders fan out on designated days to count as many individual birds as possible within a prescribed route within a larger count circle. Numbers are tallied at the end of the day and added to a massive database of species information. More information can be found on Audubon's website.

Canada Jay. This charismatic species is a resident of Maine's boreal forests.

Birds in this Guide

As of June 2021, a total of 461 bird species have been positively identified in the state of Maine. That number includes year-round residents, migrant breeders, wintering birds, birds that migrate through in spring or fall, seabirds seen only far offshore, and "vagrants," birds that show up rarely and unexpectedly, including those recorded in Maine only once.

This field guide includes 265 species, a wide swath of the possible birdlife seen in the state, and I haven't complicated things by including birds unlikely to be seen without a lot of effort. All or nearly all of the birds that commonly nest in Maine are included, as well as wintering birds and common migrants. A full list of the birds seen in Maine can be found on page 298.

For the most part, the book follows the taxonomic order as determined by the American Ornithological Society. Admittedly complicated and nonintuitive, bird taxonomy is an attempt to clarify the relationships between families of birds. I've made slight modifications, such as putting falcons close to hawks and eagles, even though those families are not closely related (falcons are more closely related to parrots, of all things), because I think it is helpful for identification purposes. Leafing through a field guide to find a particular bird can be frustrating, but blame evolution, not authors. In general, water birds come first, then land birds. With practice will come proficiency.

Each species account begins with the common name and then the bird's average length and wingspan. These numbers may not be expounded on in the text but can be useful for identification, especially when comparing two species. Downy and Hairy Woodpeckers look nearly identically, but relative size is a major clue to identification.

Species accounts generally include information about a bird's preferred habitat, its relative abundance in Maine, and the seasons in which it may be found. For many species, information is given about specific locations where the bird may be found, usually during its season of abundance. These lists are not complete and, when possible, are intended to provide locations in a variety of areas. Accounts for species whose distribution is wide generally do not mention hotspots. The tools on the "Explore Species" page of the website *eBird* (eBird. org) can help you find many more locations where certain species have been seen.

Information and tips on how to identify species are included in many of the accounts and in each photo caption. Looking for field marks will help you quickly differentiate similar-looking species, though there are plumages, variations, subspecies, and oddities that are not represented here. The vast majority of common plumages seen in Maine are included, but it's impossible to fit in everything. If you see a bird that isn't in this book, take notes and, if possible, photographs; they will be useful as you pursue an identification using the internet or larger field guides.

Each species account concludes with a note about the bird's vocalizations. These break down usually into a song—a sound made to attract a mate or defend a territory, most often in spring—and call notes, noises made to keep in touch with other birds, warn of danger, etc. Presenting bird sounds phonetically is very difficult, and sometimes borders on silly, but it can be very useful. In fact, expert birders rely on their ears more than their eyes to identify birds. Mastering bird sounds can help you find many more species by enabling you to hear them before you see them.

American Goldfinch. Learning vocalizations can help to identify species that you might not otherwise see. The frequently heard call note of the American Goldfinch sounds like "Potato chip! Potato chip!"

Parts of a Bird

PARTS OF A DUCK
This adult male American Wigeon shows most parts of a duck's body as it rests on the water. The rump is usually hidden by the flight feathers.

PARTS OF A GULL
Gulls often loaf on beaches and mudflats in large mixed flocks, making comparisons between species and ages easier.

**PARTS OF
A BIRD OF PREY**
This adult male American
Kestrel shows most parts of
a perched hawk or falcon.
The rump is usually hidden
by the flight feathers.

ear patch

crown

forehead

nape

back

bill

throat

breast

flight feathers

flank

belly

flight feathers

tail

talons

tail band

tail tip

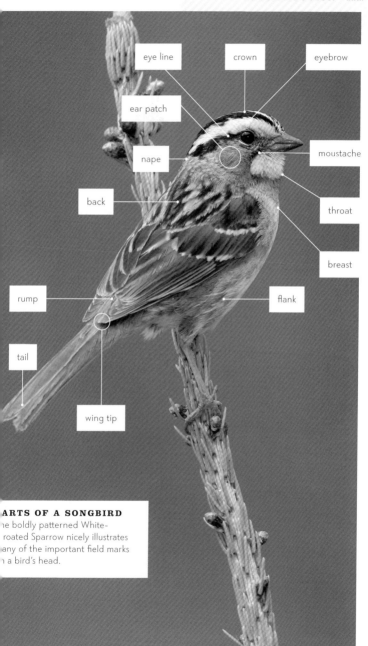

eye line

crown

eyebrow

ear patch

nape

moustache

back

throat

breast

rump

flank

tail

wing tip

PARTS OF A SONGBIRD
The boldly patterned White-
throated Sparrow nicely illustrates
many of the important field marks
on a bird's head.

Resources

By far the most important resource for the preparation of this guide was *Birds of Maine* by Peter D. Vickery. The product of decades of research and writing, the book was finished after Peter succumbed to illness by his partner Barbara Vickery and a team of friends and released posthumously by Princeton University Press in 2020. It is a masterwork, each page dense with information about every bird species ever sighted in Maine — far more than is presented here. It was an invaluable reference for me and is essential for anyone interested in Maine's avifauna.

Also incredibly useful was a cousin guide, the *American Birding Association Field Guide to Birds of Massachusetts* by Wayne R. Petersen, which served as a template and reference, as well as the *American Birding Association Field Guide to Birds of the Carolinas* by Nate Swick.

All About Birds (allaboutbirds.org) and *eBird* (ebird.org), websites operated by the Cornell Lab of Ornithology, provided reliable and concise information. *eBird*, and *Maine eBird* (ebird.org/me) in particular, are absolutely remarkable resources, assembling millions of observations that help paint a precise picture of birding in Maine and around the world.

Other works consulted include *The Sibley Guide to Birds*, Second Edition by David Allen Sibley (Knopf, 2014); *The Warbler Guide* by Tom Stephenson and Scott Whittle (Princeton University Press, 2013); *The Shorebird Guide* by Michael O'Brien, Richard Crossley, and Kevin Karlson (Houghton Mifflin, 2006); *Words for Birds* by Edward S. Gruson (Quad-rangle Books, 1972); *Gulls of the World* by Klaus Malling Olsen (Princeton University Press, 2018); and Bob Duchesene's website *Maine Birding Trail* (mainebirdingtrail.com).

Maine Birding Trail is an excellent place to start for any resident or visitor looking to plan a birding trip to Maine, as it presents information on locations, seasons, tours, festivals, cruises, and other helpful tips.

Maine Audubon (maineaudubon.org) is another good place to

start. An independent organization, it has worked since 1843 to protect wildlife and wildlife habitat across the state. It operates eight wildlife sanctuaries, which are free and open to the public: Gilsland Farm in Falmouth, Fields Pond in Holden, East Point in Biddeford Pool, Borestone Mountain near Monson, Scarborough Marsh Audubon Center in Scarborough, Mast Landing in Freeport, Josephine Newman in Georgetown, and Hamilton in West Bath. Visit Maine Audubon's website for information about events and programming.

The following Maine Audubon chapters provide additional trips and services across the state:

Downeast (downeastaudubon.org), in Hancock County, including Mount Desert Island and Acadia National Park

Merrymeeting (merrymeeting.maineaudubon.org), in the Brunswick area

Mid-Coast (midcoast.maineaudubon.org), the Camden, Boothbay, China, and Bucksport area

Penobscot Valley (pvc.maineaudubon.org), from Bucksport through Bangor to Millinocket

Fundy (fundy.maineaudubon.org), covering all of Washington County

Western Maine (western.maineaudubon.org), covering Franklin County and the Western Mountains, based in Farmington

York County (yorkcountyaudubon.org), covering York County, based at the Wells Reserve at Laudholm Farm

Two additional bird clubs are active in Maine:

Maine Young Birders Club (maineyoungbirders.org), based in York County but ranging all over the state, hosting monthly trips for young birders

Stanton Bird Club (stantonbirdclub.org), founded in 1919, hosting events, talks, and birding outings in the Lewiston area

American Birding Association

Field Guide to Birds of Maine

Brant
Branta bernicla

L 23" | **WS** 45"

Smaller, black-and-white cousins of the more numerous
Canada Goose, Brant are rarely found away from salt water.
Typically seen in small flocks feeding on aquatic plants in the
shallows or grazing on short grass close to the shore. Brant
are winter residents along the Maine coast, lingering into
May before migrating to breeding grounds in the Arctic. Less
common in Maine than in southern New England and the Mid-
Atlantic, but can give accommodating views at regular haunts
along the south coast, especially Kettle Cove and Two Lights
State Park in Cape Elizabeth, and Biddeford Pool. Mostly
silent, but may give a loud, rolling *ronk*.

Dark on the water with whitish sides and white
backside. White "necklace" may be more or less
prominent in some individuals or in certain
conditions, and is absent altogether in juveniles.

Canada Goose

Branta canadensis

L 30-43" | **WS** 50-67"

The large and abundant Canada Goose is a familiar sight on almost any freshwater body during a Maine summer, though it wasn't always that way. Ceaseless sport-hunting had extirpated breeding Canada Geese from the state in the 1800s, but 20th century reintroductions and protections for migratory flocks have helped them rebound. Resident birds are supplemented in spring and fall by migrant flocks moving between wintering areas in breeding grounds further north. Migrant flocks staging in agricultural fields in fall can number in the thousands, particularly in Aroostook County. In winter, Canada Geese flee the ice in search of open water, which may include any ice-free sections of rivers or lakes but is most commonly in sheltered bays along the sea coast. Flies in their famous "V" formation, with individuals in both airborne and grounded flocks producing a near-constant *hh-ONK*.

White backside stands out in flying birds, though their frequent honking often announces their presence before they're seen. Large brown bird with distinctive black neck and white cheek patch.

Wood Duck

Aix sponsa

L 20" | **WS** 27"

The regal Wood Duck is a common, though often difficult to see, resident of swamps, ponds, and other water bodies with standing trees or emergent vegetation. Its name derives from its habitat of nesting not on the ground but in tree cavities, often in water bodies enlarged by beavers. Thankfully, they also readily take to appropriately-placed nest boxes, a fact which helped aid their recovery in Maine after overhunting dwindled their numbers nearly completely in the early 1900s. Migrant birds arrive in late March or early April and stay into October. Overwintering birds are rare but regular, usually among large flocks of Mallard or American Black Duck. Wood Ducks are shy and quick to take to the air, with female birds giving an alarmed, rising *oooeeeeeep*; Call of the male is an insistent, two-parted *woo-EEK*.

Males are absolutely stunning, sporting a dignified plumage of mahogany, tan, white, and iridescent green, and a drooping head crest.

Flight is swift and direct, oven low. White belly and white chin patch are helpful for identification.

Females show a crested gray head with distinctive white teardrop-shaped feathering around the eye.

Blue-winged Teal
Spatula discors

L 15" | **WS** 23"

A small, dabbling duck most commonly encountered in Maine during spring or fall migration, often in association with Green-winged Teal or Mallards. Spring birds move through in small flocks from late March through April, and are most often encountered at vegetated wetlands, including Scarborough Marsh, Weskeag Marsh or Penjajawog Marsh. An infrequent breeder in the state, more common in northern or eastern Maine. Spring males are easily identified by a large white crescent between their bill and their eye, and in flight both sexes show helpful, sky blue patches on the tops of their wings. Identification gets trickier for late summer and fall birds, as both sexes sport drabber plumage. If wing patches aren't visible, look for the large, all-black bills to help distinguish from female Mallard or American Black Duck, and pale face patch and larger size to help distinguish from Green-winged Teal. Male gives a repeated, chirping *peep!* while females give a barking *squawk*.

Stately spring male has blue-gray head with bright white crescent, spotted flanks, and white patches near rump. Blue wing patches are hidden when wings are folded, though sometimes telltale flashes of color are visible. Nondescript female (upper left) shows a large black bill, pale face, and overall grayish tone.

Northern Shoveler

Spatula clypeata

L 19" | **WS** 31"

The most prominent identification feature for these dabbling
ducks is their long, spoon-shaped bill—their "shovel"—which
they sweep back and forth through shallow water to capture
invertebrates. These uncommon ducks are at their most
abundant during spring and fall migration where they may
be found stopping over on lakes or marshes, usually near the
coast. The species regularly breeds on Lake Josephine and
Christina Reservoir in Aroostook County, and in recent years
also on Stratton Island, in Cumberland County off Old Orchard
Beach. Their massive bills—black on breeding males and orange
on females and nonbreeding males—are a useful identification
feature in any sex or plumage, but the green head, white breast
and bold rusty sides of a male in breeding plumage are also prominent, especially in flight. Courting males give a grunted *cluck*.

The male's white breast may
stand out most prominently
from a distance, and the large
black bill gives the bird a
distinctively front-heavy look.

Gadwall

Mareca strepera

L 20" | **WS** 33"

An understated dabbling duck, the Gadwall is uncommonly encountered in Maine. Gadwall are most often encountered at migratory stopover sites in spring, usually shallow ponds or marshes such as Scarborough Marsh, Great Salt Bay Wildlife Preserve in Damariscotta, or Penjajawoc Marsh in Penobscot County. The species breeds in small numbers around the state, though perhaps nowhere reliably, save for Lake Josephine in Aroostook County. Gray breeding plumage males are most readily identified by their black rumps. Females, juveniles, and nonbreeding plumage males can be separated from similar species by plain face and, if visible, a small triangle of white feathers on the flank, which is visible in flight as a white square of feathers where the wing meets the body. Male gives a distinctive pig-like *beep* during courtship.

Male in breeding plumage shows a gray body and puffy vbrown head. Whitish feathers towards tail and black rear section are distinctive.

Female resembles female Mallard but with high, steep forehead lacking a bold eyeline. Triangular white patch (the bird's inner flight feathers) sometimes visible towards the rear.

American Wigeon

Mareca americana

L 20" | **WS** 33"

This tidy duck is an uncommon migrant through the state
in spring and fall, with a few northern and central breeding
locations. They begin arriving in small numbers at coastal
and near-coast locations in mid-March—Biddeford Pool,
Scarborough Marsh, Gilsland Farm Audubon Center, Bass
Harbor Marsh on Mt. Desert Island, and inland to Sebasticook Lake—before continuing north by the end of April. A few
breeding records in central Maine and a regular breeder in
parts of Aroostook County. An active feeder, swimming with
a distinctive leaned-forward posture, American Wigeon pluck
vegetation off the water surface and occasionally graze on
fields. In flight, note white bellies and underwing, bright white
upper wing patches, and pointed tail. Makes utter a distinctive
descending whistle, a sort of soft, wheezing quack: *weew-
WEEW-weew-weew*.

Bright white forehead stripe is the most distinctive feature of a male, and helps with ID from a distance. Green stripe on the side of the head and white patch alongside side also distinctive.

Females and nonbreeding males are not distinctive, but the round, plain head and short, black-tipped blue bill are helpful.

Mallard

Anas platyrhynchos

L 23" | **WS** 35"

The Mallard is the most common and widespread duck in Maine, found in just about any body of open water in any season, including city parks, lakes and rivers, coastal bays, and flooded fields. This duck was rare in the state a century ago and was not known to nest in the state until 1949, but the bird's tolerance of human development and a ban on spring hunting has lifted them to their current ubiquity. Females and nonbreeding males are drab and can pose an identification challenge with the closely-related American Black Duck. Confusing things further, the two species frequently hybridize, resulting in individual birds with plumage characteristics of both species. Barnyard escapees or other domestic breeds can also make their way into the gene pool, confusing identification further. For identification of "pure" females, look for orange bill with black splotches, tan body, and deep blue wing patch with white border. Females give the classic *quack-quack-quack* though nearly identical to that of the American Black Duck.

Females are light brown with an orange bill with black splotches. The white lines bordering the blue wing patch are key to help distinguish from American Black Duck.

Handsome breeding plumage of a male Mallard characterized by green head, white necklace, and curly black tail feathers.

American Black Duck

Anas rubripes

L 22″ | **WS** 36″

While declining in the southerly parts of its range, due in no small part to competition and hybridization with the closely-related Mallard, Maine's American Black Duck populations is relatively stable. Habits and habitats are similar to the Mallard. Most abundant in calm coastal coves, coastal mudflats, and salt water estuaries, where it regularly mixes with Mallards. Pairs can be found breeding throughout the state in summer, from the coast to mountain lakes in western Maine to Aroostook County. Males and females similar except for slight differences in the color of the bill -- olive green in females and yellow-green in males -- and other minor differences. Males do not have a flashy plumage like their Mallard cousins, and are instead separated from female Mallards by deep chocolate body, green (not orange or yellow) bill, and lack of white border on purple wing patch. Voice is a Mallard-like quacking.

Underwings are bright silvery-white, which stands out against the dark belly and upper wings. Shape and flight style otherwise like Mallard.

Clean dark brown throughout the body, contrasting with pale brown head. Dull green bill also distinctive.

Northern Pintail

Anas acuta

L 20–30" | **WS** 35"

A long-necked duck admired for its sleek grace, the Northern
Pintail is a worldwide species uncommonly encountered in
Maine, mostly in spring and fall migration. Has bred in Maine,
near Lake Josephine in Aroostook County, and occasionally over-winters along the coast, usually in the company of
Mallards. Spring migrants arrive as early as mid-March, and
prefer open wetlands along the coast. Southbound migrants
peak in September in the same areas, or occasionally in flooded
farm fields. Breeding male is a showstopper with a clean brown
and white patterned head and a long black tail. Females are
inconspicuous—all-over tan with a gray bill. Males utter short
chatters and whistles, while female quacks like a Mallard.

The elegant breeding male Northern Pintail is
set apart by its brown head, long neck, white
breast, and long tail feathers off a black
rump.A thin, white "trailing edge" on the back
of wings is a useful identification point in
flight, as are the long neck and slender wings.

Female is perhaps most notable for its lack
of markings, lacking the eye-stripe and wing
patches of female Mallards or American
Black Ducks. Tan all over with a dark bill.

Green-winged Teal

Anas crecca

L 14″ | **WS** 22″

The charming Green-winged Teal is the smallest of the
dabbling ducks in Maine. They're boldly-patterned when seen
in the open—the males with maroon heads and a green streak
beginning at the eye—but their coloration helps them blend
into the banks of wetlands and tidal marshes, where they're
easy to overlook. Breeds in small numbers around the state
but most regularly seen in spring and fall migration in tidal
marshes or shallow lakes with exposed mud. Swims excitedly,
typically in small flocks, but their retiring nature adds to their
inconspicuousness. Male gives a short peeping sound often
compared to an amphibian, and female delivers a short *quack*.

Small gray duck with smart red and green head pattern. Thin white vertical stripe on the side
is useful from afar, and distinguishes "American" Green-winged Teal from "Eurasian"
Green-winged Teal (which lack the stripe), a subspecies rarely recorded in Maine.

Female nondescript: small and brown
with a dark bill. Green wing-patch is
diagnostic if visible (it's often not, or
hard to see from a distance).

Canvasback

Aythya valisineria

L 20" | **WS** 33"

A large and distinguished duck, the Canvasback is a rare sight in Maine. Recorded occasionally in spring, fall, and winter, most often near the mouths of rivers around Casco Bay or larger migrant stopover lakes such as Sebasticook Lake or Sabattus Pond. A diving duck -- not a dabbler -- Canvasback will disappear underwater to forage for plants and mollusks. Best identified by large maroon head sloping down along a black bill. Bright white sides contrast with black chest and rump on breeding males, the plumage most commonly seen in Maine. Calls include a harsh grating growl, but Canvasback rarely vocalize away from their breeding grounds in the western U.S. and Canada.

A powerful-looking duck, with deep red head and bright white sides. The dark forehead sloping smoothly down to the tip of the black bill is a useful identification feature from a distance.

Female tan, with darker brown on the breast and neck. Large black bill and forehead slope distinctive.

Ring-necked Duck
Aythya collaris

L 17" | **WS** 25"

A ring around the neck is one of the least-helpful identification features of the Ring-necked Duck, a species high on the list of "Confusingly-named Birds." The ring is there, of course, as a faint reddish gloss seen only in certain light, but it's difficult to see. Instead, focus your attention on the blue-gray bill outlined in white and the white "spur" sticking up along the side of the breast. Ring-necked Ducks are one of the most common migratory ducks in Maine, often seen in flocks of a dozen to more than a hundred as they move through shallow inland lakes and ponds close to ice-out in early spring, peaking in April. Ringnecks are fairly common breeders throughout northern and eastern Maine, with some sites in the western mountains and near the Mid-coast. Perturbed females utter a hoarse *urrh urrh*, and males utter short squeaks and barks, though rarely heard.

Males can be confused with other pale-sided ducks such as scaup, but combination of patterned bill, white side spur, and peaked head are distinctive. Faint red neck ring, however, is not useful for field identification.

Female Ring-necked Ducks are pale brown overall, with distinctive white ring around the bill, white patch where the bill meets the face, and white eye-ring.

Greater Scaup

Aythya marila

L 15-22" | **WS** 30"

The Greater Scaup and its close cousin the Lesser Scaup are famously difficult to tell apart from one another. The most useful distinguishing field mark -- the shape of the head -- can vary based on the activity and angle of the bird, so proceed with caution. Greater Scaup are an uncommon migrant in early spring and late fall, found in mixed duck flocks on inland lakes and ponds. They're most commonly found along the coast in winter, both as individual birds and in flocks with hundreds of birds, in places like Marginal Way in Ogunquit, Maquoit Bay in Brunswick, and Hadley Point in Bar Harbor. Habitat can be a clue to identification: Lesser Scaup are almost never found on salt water, while Greater are less common inland, except during migration. Both species have endured steep population declines in recent decades due, it's believed, to water pollution at their urban wintering areas, habitat degradation, and hunting.

Male. Greater Scaup have lower, longer, gently sloped heads than Lesser Scaup. Green iridescence on head seen only in the right light. In flight, look for bright white stripe on the wings, more extensive than in the Lesser Scaup.

Females show large white patch behind bill. Brownish overall with blue-gray bill. Note sloping head shape.

Lesser Scaup

Aythya affinis

L 16" | **WS** 29"

Very similar to Greater Scaup, the Lesser Scaup can be distinguished -- with care -- by its taller head and sharper transition between crown and neck. Considered more common inla nd during migration than Greater Scaup and less common along the coast, though both species can occur in either location. Generally later migrants than Greater Scaup, peaking in April and November (as opposed to March and October) at waterfowl hotspots such as Sanford Lagoons, Sabattus Pond, Cobbosseecontee Lake, and Sebasticook Lake. Lesser Scaup populations are experiencing similar declines as Greater, for the same reasons.

Head is narrower at the top, with a sharper transition between crown and neck, sometimes appearing as a bump or tuft. More prominent barring on back and darker head color than very similar Greater Scaup, but these field marks are unreliable for separating the two. Thin white wing stripe in flight.

Head shape again the most helpful marking, showing the short flat-topped head with sharper angle to the neck.

Common Eider
Somateria mollissima

L 24" | **WS** 38"

Common Eiders are the largest duck species in North America, and may be found floating in near-shore waters in any season. While occasionally seen on inland lakes during spring and fall migration as some individuals move between breeding areas in the Gulf of St. Lawrence, Common Eiders are ubiquitous along the entire seacoast, seen slowly swimming offshore, resting on rocks, or diving to the seabed for mussels and crustaceans. Numbers peak in winter as northern migrants seek ice-free waters, and "rafts" of over one hundred birds are common at favorite sites. Common Eiders breed on rocky, treeless islands up and down the coast. While still a common sight, Common Eider numbers have steadily declined in recent decades, likely due in part to changing benthic conditions in the warming Gulf of Maine. Tidy, black-and-white breeding-age males are relatively easy to identify, but mottled young birds and dark-brown females may pose a challenge and are best sorted by the combination of large side and sloping forehead.

Male. Common Eiders in breeding plumage are a sharp black and white with large, bright yellow bill and mossy green patches on the top of the neck.

Female is rusty to chocolate brown, with few markings to help in flight except for large size and sloped forehead.

Young birds and nonbreeding males are irregularly patterned with splotchy white, brown, and black.

Harlequin Duck

Histrionicus histrionicus

L 17" | **WS** 24"

Harlequin Ducks are a true standout along the coast, where it seems that some combination of black, white, gray, or brown is the default. A bright, smoky-blue body patterned with gaudy daubs of white, navy, and chestnut, the male Harlequin looks like nothing else on the water. A winter-only visiter, tight flocks of these small ducks are never found far from their favorite areas, including Cape Neddick, Two Lights State Park, Schoodic Point, and the island in outer Penobscot Bay. In summer, Maine's birds migrate to Quebec or Greenland to nest along fast-moving mountain rivers. Female Harlequins are brown with a telltale white spot on the sides of the head. Utter distinctive whistles, like a dog's squeaky toy.

Showstopping male is unmistakable. Small and chunky with chestnut flanks, white face and ear spot, long tail.

Bufflehead

Bucephala albeola

L 14" | **WS** 21"

A rubber ducky crossed with an oreo cookie, the tiny Bufflehead makes a welcome return to Maine's coastal seas in early fall and stays into late spring, moving northward soon after ice out. Named for the bulbous noggins, Bufflehead can be found on almost any shallow, nearshore water in the winter, diving continuously and popping back up the surface nearby. Typically seen in small groups of males and females together, but can congregate in favored areas such as the mouth of the Presumpscot River in Falmouth, upper Penobscot Bay, around Mount Desert Island, and others. Males engage in entertaining head-bobbing courtship displays through the winter and spring, and Bufflehead are often seen on inland lakes during late spring migration, though breeding in the state has never been confirmed.

Tiny, but brilliant white on head and sides can be seen from a great distance. Iridescent sheen on head only evident at close range.

Females brownish with distinctive white cheek patch, most always seen in small flocks with males nearby.

Black Scoter

Melanitta americana

L 19" | **WS** 33"

The Black Scoter is the smallest of the three scoter species regularly seen in Maine. Like Surf and White-winged, it is most common in winter and can be found in large mixed species flocks up and down the coast, with higher concentrations seen around Mount Desert Island and south of Rockland. Migrates in large numbers in April and May up the coast before turning north in New Brunswick and passing over northern Maine before making their way to freshwater lakes on the tundra. Severe weather can interrupt these migrations and result in sea duck "fallouts" on lakes in Aroostook County which may include all three scoters. Small numbers of young birds remain off the coast through the summer. Male Black Scoters are readily identified by the bulbous yellow knob on their bill, and glossy black body. Females' curving white cheek patch distinctive. Male scoters utter a plaintive, mourning whistle, and their wings whistle in flight.

Male is all black with lemony bulb perched on black bill.

Both sexes have silvery wing linings which may be seen in flight.

Brownish female distinguished from other female scoters by extensive pale cheeks contrasting with dark cap and neck.

Surf Scoter
Melanitta perspicillata

L 21" | **WS** 30"

One of three closely related species of black sea duck, most
common in winter, most easily separated by comparison of
white markings (or lack thereof) on the heads of male birds.
Surf Scoters are common along the entire coast in winter,
often lingering into late May before migrating to the breeding
grounds on the Canadian tundra. Oversummering birds not
uncommon, particularly around offshore islands. The large
bulbous white-and-yellow bill and white patches on forehead
and neck are distinctive on males. Females of all three scoter
species more challenging, female Surf Scoters best separated
by vertical white patch behind bill. Most often seen diving
for mollusks among the waves, or flying fast and low over the
water, as all scoters do.

Bulbous, colorful bill and white
head patches are distinctive

Brownish female best
separated from similar
female White-winged Scoter
by vertically-oriented white
patch behind the bill and
lack of white wing stripe.

White-winged Scoter

Melanitta deglandi

L 21" | **WS** 32"

This species' namesake wing patches can be seen from a great distance, making the White-winged Scoter the easiest of the three scoters to identify in flight. The white patch can usually be seen when swimming, too, as a thin line or small triangle along the rear. Our largest scoter, White-winged Scoters are common along Maine's rocky coast in winter, becoming more common along the southern coast. Numbers peak during spring and fall migrations when strings of hundreds of birds may be seen flying low over the water. As with other scoters, it feeds by diving to pry molluscs from the bottom or pluck crustaceans.

On the water, glamorous white tear-drop patch around eye is distinctive. White wing patch often visible along flanks, though sometimes obscured.

Females are large and dark brown, with two white blotches on the head and face. White wing patch often visible while swimming, and conspicuous when the species is in flight or spreads wings to dive.

Long-tailed Duck
Clangula hyemalis

L 19" | **WS** 28"

The Long-tailed Duck is a small but dashing sea duck found in small flocks all along Maine's sea coast in winter. The species rests offshore and flies daily to nearshore waters to dive for food. Though small and often overlooked, wintering Long-tailed Ducks can be found in almost coastal waters, from calm estuaries like Back Cove in Portland to rougher ocean waters like those found off Schoodic Peninsula or Biddeford Pool. Plumage can be cryptic, and small flocks are often a confusing jumble of whites, browns, blacks, and tans. The thin brown tail feathers of the male are diagnostic but sometimes difficult to see, but the combination of white sides, neck and crown with dark cheek is distinctive. Females lack long tail, and show a white face with dark cheek and crown. Perhaps the species' most endearing trait is its loud, three-part yodel, *onk onk owlEEP!*, an evocative accompaniment to a chilly winter visit to the Maine coast.

Lovely winter plumage male shows rich dark-and-light patterning. Long tail obvious when seen, but often held low and out of sight.

Winter female in flight note small size, white head and white rump patches.

Winter female mottled brown and white, with white face framed by crown and dark cheek patch.

Common Goldeneye

Bucephala clangula

L 18" | **WS** 31"

The stately Common Goldeneye is something of an in-state snowbird, spending the winters on ice-free water along the coast and moving into the boreal north and the western mountains in spring to breed. They breed in tree cavities near water and seem to prefer smaller lakes and ponds with forested edges. Common Goldeneye will linger in fall later than most other migratory ducks, and will wait until the encroaching ice forces them south, often appearing near the coast in late November. Most common in winter south of Mount Desert Island, the species may be seen engaging in courtship displays along shallow bays and harbors, such as Perkins Cove in Ogunquit, the Royal River in Yarmouth, and Rockland Harbor, to name a few. The ringing flutter given by their wings on take-off tagged them with the colloquial name "whistlers," but they're otherwise quiet except for grunted peents given during elaborate, head-throwing courtship displays.

Stark white sides, black back, peaked head with round white patch distinctive.

Female is gray with a brownish head, dark bill often tipped with yellow.

Barrow's Goldeneye

Bucephala islandica

L 18" | **WS** 28"

A Threatened species in Maine, the Barrow's Goldeneye is the less-numerous lookalike of the Common Goldeneye. Barrow's Goldeneye do not breed in the state, but they occupy the same winter habitats and often intermingle with Commons. May appear at any ice-free river, bay, or estuary, but regular in deep winter along the Penobscot River from Orono to Bucksport, the mouth of the Harraseeket River in Yarmouth, and the lower Saco River. Separation from Common Goldeneye a challenge, especially for female and young birds. Head shape is useful in all plumages, as Barrow's have steeper foreheads and smaller bills than Commons.

Males show distinctive crescent-shaped white spot behind bill, as compared to the round shape on Commons, and also show more black along the sides and a black "spur" towards the breast.

Female usually shows dark-tipped all or mostly-yellow/orange bill in winter, but can be variable. Smaller bill side and steeper forehead also useful to separate from Common Goldeneye.

Hooded Merganser

Lophodytes cucullatus

L 18" | **WS** 24"

The smallest of Maine's three species of merganser, a group of diving ducks which use their thin, serrated bills to snag wriggly fish. The Hooded Merganser, with its brilliant fan-shaped crest, is a standout. Breeds nearly statewide, nesting in tree cavities and nest boxes near small freshwater bodies or rivers. Hooded Merganser numbers have greatly increased over the previous decades hunting pressure eased, as forests regenerated along lakes and ponds, and as beavers returned to create new habitat. Less common but not unusual in winter at ice-free rivers and estuaries all along the coast. Numbers peak overall during spring and fall migration as birds move between more southerly wintering areas. Usually quiet, but males give a drawn-out croak during courtship and around nest sites, and the wings both sexes emit a high twittering during flight.

Black and white with chestnut flanks. Crest may be raised or lowered, giving the head shape a very different profile.

When raised fully, the male's crest can be seen from a great distance.

Female is brown all over, with brown crest that may also be raised or lowered. Thin bill, as with all mergansers, with yellow below. Thin white stripe on upper wing visible in flight.

Common Merganser

Mergus merganser

L 25" | **WS** 34"

This large, sleek merganser is a year-round resident, breeding across the state and pushed by encroaching ice to the coasts in winter. Bright white sides advertise their presence on lakes, fast-moving rivers, and shallow coastal bays in summer, notably present as breeders in popular destinations like Acadia National Park and Baxter State Park, where they seek tree cavities, hollow logs, tangled tree roots, and other nesting holes. Common Mergansers linger in winter, often seen in small flocks on half-frozen lakes or rivers, but most common on salt water from Mount Desert through the southern coast. Smooth head helps distinguish male Common Mergansers from shaggy-crested Red-breasted Mergansers, and larger size and prominent white chin patch relevant to separate females of the two species.

A stately duck, with bright white sides, glossy green head and bright red bill. White body is obvious in flight, as are large white wing patches.

Female is brown headed, with spikey crest and prominent white chin patch. Common Mergansers are long and low-slung in the water.

Red-breasted Merganser

Mergus serrator

L 23" | **WS** 28"

The Red-breasted Merganser is a very common sight along the coast in winter. Migrants enter the state in late September and October, fleeing the onset of winter in their northern breeding grounds, and are seemingly on every patch of salt water all up and down the coast by November. They dive near constantly, darting around underwater in pursuit of minnows, killifish, herring, silversides, and a variety of other aquatic prey. Red-breasted Mergansers slowly return north beginning in March and may occasionally be found inland during migration. Though a few individuals may remain along the coast through the summer, the bulk of the population is gone by June. Red-breasted Mergansers are rarely heard vocalizing in Maine.

Shaggy crest and messy, multicolored plumage give the impression of a teenager just having gotten out of bed. Red breast often appears dark, or brown, but is distinctive among other coastal ducks in winter.

All mergansers fly fast, with shallow wingbeats and heads held out straight.

Browner and shaggier than similar female Common Merganser; with less-obvious white patch on throat and smaller crest.

Ruddy Duck

Oxyura jamaicensis

L 15" | **WS** 23"

The squat Ruddy Duck is an uncommon migrant and rare breeder in the state, with its peak numbers coming in fall. Bold red, white, black, and blue breeding plumage of male rarely seen in Maine, instead look for the drabber gray winter plumage, offset by a bright white cheek, on large ponds in late fall, often in the company of other migrant waterfowl. Favorite migratory stopover sites include the wastewater treatment facility in Sanford, Grondin Pond in Cape Elizabeth, Sabattus Pond in Sabattus, and Sebasticook Lake in Newport. The first breeding record of Ruddy Duck in the state came in 2005 on Lake Josephine in Aroostook County, and they have continued on and off since then. Most useful field mark might be their long tail, often held stiffly behind them like a folding fan.

Winter plumage male is gray brown with dark cap and bright white cheek. Still tail held high a very helpful feature, especially when bird is asleep on the water with head tucked away.

Female is brown with dark line across cheek and telltale tall tail.

Ruffed Grouse

Bonasa umbellus

L 17"   **WS** 22"

Known locally as a "partridge," the well-camouflaged Ruffed Grouse is widespread in the state, with an estimated population of around 1.5 million. They may be found in mixed forests in every county and even some offshore islands, though most numerous in northern Maine. One of Maine's most popular game birds, the state holds a hunting season between late September through the end of the year. Locating these cryptic grouse can be difficult, and many encounters begin when a hiker unwittingly gets too close to an unseen bird and it bursts in a flapping fury. Once the observer's heart stops racing, the bird may be found just a short ways away, perched low in a tree. On the other hand, there are regular reports of overly friendly Ruffed Grouse, which appear tame or even tag along after hikers, perhaps due to the territoriality of the birds. The bird is perhaps most famous for their "drumming" displays, performed March into June, where make birds beat their wings to produce an accelerating series of concussive thumps, like someone starting a faraway lawnmower. During these displays the birds also spread their tail and spread a collar of feathers around their neck; their namesake "ruff."

A medium-sized, chunky grouse. Color ranged from gray to reddish, with extensive barring and spotting acting as excellent camouflage. Sexes similar.

Spruce Grouse

Falcipennis canadensis

L 16" | **WS** 22"

The Spruce Grouse is a mythic bird of dense spruce-fir forests in northern and western Maine. They're a famously tame species, colloquially called the "Fool Hen," permitting the lucky observer to get prolonged looks as they eat fir, spruce, and pine needles—and the unlucky observer to walk right past them without noticing. Their coniferous diet makes them unpalatable, and there is no hunting season for Spruce Grouse in Maine. Instead, a changing climate appears to be their biggest threat, and the species is absent from their former territories in Midcoast Maine, and is anecdotally becoming scarcer in far western Maine. Typically quiet, but can utter a variety of sounds, including soft clucks from females, and tail-whooshing sounds and occasional double-thumps from courting males.

Handsome male shows black throat and red "comb" above eye. Female, not pictured, heavily barred, brown and rufous. Both sexes darker than Ruffed Grouse.

Wild Turkey

Meleagris gallopavo

L 42" | **WS** 53"

Believe it or not, the iconic native Wild Turkey was extirpated
from Maine in the late 1880s. Reintroduction efforts stalled
through the 20th century but efforts in the Midcoast and York
County took hold in the past few decades, and these huge
grouse are once again common throughout Maine, including
many coastal islands, with the exception of the densely-
forested north. A popular game bird, the state hosts both spring
and fall hunting seasons, with exact dates varying by location. Can be found in a variety of habitats, including suburban
neighborhoods, agricultural fields and other large clearings,
and open oak woods. Look for the puffed-out courtship display
of males, accompanied by famous gobbling and strutting, in
early spring. Flies into and out of trees to roost at night.

A male in full display is unmistakable.
Note bright red and blue skin on
bare face and neck, scraggly "beard,"
glossy black feathers on body, and
orange-tipped tail feathers. Bare
parts of females, juveniles, and
non-breeding males are less colorful.

Common Loon

Gavia immer

L 26-36" | **WS** 41-52"

One of Maine's most beloved birds, the intricate and powerful Common Loon can be found in the state year-round. Breeding-age birds migrate in early spring to ponds and lakes across Maine, returning to an established territory that they vigor-ously defend for years. Common Loons nest close to the water's edge (they have difficulty on land, and so don't go far), making nests susceptible to washout from boat wake and other distur-bances. Plumage during this time is exquisite: pristine and precise black and white checkering, and vocalizations are a soundtrack to a Maine summer. Male Common Loons emit an eerie yodel to advertise and defend territories, and mournful wails, often at dusk, are used to communicate between partners and pairs. Floaty, laughing "tremolo" call given in flight or in distress. Common Loons flee the encroaching ice in fall and are a common sight along the coast in both nearshore and offshore waters all winter, with many younger individuals remaining for the summer. Winter plumage dark with white throat and neck, large size, blocky head and heavy bill useful to separate from cormorants and grebes.

Breeding plumage unmistakeable, an elegant suit of sharply contrasting black and white. Note block head with forehead bump, large dark bill held horizontally.

Young birds are dependent on adults for food for about eight weeks, never straying far from parents and often hitching a ride right on their backs.

Adults in winter and immatures are blackish above and white below, with blocky head and large, horizontally-held bill, and jagged border between dark and light on the neck useful to distinguish from other seabirds.

Red-throated Loon

Gavia stellata

L 24" | **WS** 43"

A daintier cousin of our familiar Common Loon, the Red-throated Loon is primarily a winter visitor, escaping its frozen freshwater breeding ponds in the high arctic for the Atlantic and Pacific coasts. As all loons, the Red-throated Loon is a champion fish-catcher, propelling itself underwater with its large, rear-mounted legs and snagging fish in its bill. Relatively common anywhere on the coast in winter, especially south of Mount Desert Island. May appear in large numbers during spring and fall migration passing the tips of coastal peninsulas. Namesake red-throated breeding plumage infrequently seen in Maine, though possible on lingering spring migrants and for rare oversummering individuals, most birds show white-faced non-breeding plumage. Longer body and shorter neck than grebes, and thin bill often held high, somewhat snobbily, is a useful field mark.

Smaller, slimmer, and paler than winter Common Loon, with bright white face, speckled back, and thin bill held aloft.

Pied-billed Grebe
Podilymbus podiceps

L 13" | **WS** 21"

A fairly common but easily overlooked summer resident, breeding on quiet ponds and grassy wetlands. Known breeder at more than a dozen marshes across the state, including Messalonskee Lake in Belgrade, Great Salt Bay Wildlife Preserve in Damariscotta, and Essex Woods in Bangor. Possible in migration at any number of freshwater ponds, typically near the cost in southern Maine. Small and brown overall, with namesake black-and-white bill, most often seen near grassy edges, giving for aquatic prey. Song a loud series of laughing barks or toots which accelerates then decelerates.

n breeding plumage mousy brown with black throat patch and patterned white bill with black band.
Nonbreeding birds similar but lack black bill band and black throat patch.

Horned Grebe

Podiceps auritus

L 14" | **WS** 24"

A small, delicate waterbird, the Horned Grebe is a common winter visitor to the Maine Coast. Small flocks appear in October in nearshore coastal waters, bays, and inlets, already in their muted black-and-white nonbreeding plumage. Small size, straight neck, and pointed bill distinguish them from ducks, and clean demarcation between black cap and white cheeks separates from similar Eared Grebe, a rare vagrant to Maine waters from the western U.S. Lingering spring migrants may achieve breeding plumage, showing attractive black and gold head pattern. Inclined flight posture, small size, and white patch on upperwing useful in flight.

Smudgy dark gray overall, with white cheeks contrasting with darker cap.

Red-necked Grebe

Podiceps grisegena

L 20" | **WS** 24-35"

Our largest regularly-occurring grebe, the Red-necked Grebe is most common as a fall migrant and winter resident. It's yellow bill is longer and heavier than Horned Grebe, while long neck helpful to distinguish from Common Loon. Fall migrants arrive along the coast as early as late August, often in large flocks at favored sites like Frenchman's Bay, Penobscot Bay, and off Mount Desert Island. Some of these birds may arrive in their red-necked breeding plumage, though most birds seen in fall and through the winter show a nondescript, smudgy gray and white, with pale ear patch contrasting against dark crown. Common in winter along the length of the Maine coast, particularly off rocky promontories like East Point in Biddeford Pool or Reid State Park in Georgetown. Numbers reduce as the winter wears on before peaking again in spring as birds move to breeding grounds to the northwest. Generally silent when in Maine waters.

Some birds may show remnants of red neck as they molt into winter plumage, which is gray-brown overall with gently contrasting black and white on the head. Heavy yellow bill often held at a downward angle.

Wilson's Storm-Petrel

Oceanites oceanicus

L 7" | **WS** 16"

Brown, swallow-sized birds with bright white rumps, Wilson's Storm-Petrels visit offshore waters in the Gulf of Maine during our summer, while their breeding grounds on Antarctica and its surrounding islands are cloaked in winter. Considered one of the most numerous birds on Earth, spotting a Wilson's Storm-Petrel is nevertheless a rare treat in Maine, typically achieved via a whale watching cruise, dedicated pelagic birding trip, or, with luck, ferry boats en route to Vinalhaven, Monhegan, or other offshore waters. Remarkable foraging behavior sees the birds hovering inches above the sea, their dangling feet skipping along the surface as they scan for floating morsels.

Small and dark chocolate brown with prominent white rump and pale band across the wing. Distinguished from Leach's Storm-Petrel by blunted wings, floaty slight style, long legs.

Leach's Storm-Petrel

Hydrobates monorhis

L 8" | **WS** 18"

As many as 10,000 of these secretive storm-petrels breed on rocky, treeless islands off the Maine coast. However, coming and going from their underground burrows only at night imparts a mysterious air around the birds, even to biologists working on breeding colonies. Bounding, erratic flight with deep wingbeats reminiscent of a moth, or a Common Nighthawk. Generally seen further offshore than Wilson's Storm-Petrel, and only expected in Maine from a whale watching trip or dedicated offshore birding cruise. Declining numbers in Maine and around North America tied to rising sea temperatures.

Dark brown back often bisects or notches into white rump creating a V shape, though variable and difficult to see. Long wings, deeply notched tail, and bounding flight style help distinguish from Wilson's.

Cory's Shearwater

Calonectris diomedea

L 19" | **WS** 46"

Shearwaters are a group of oceanic birds with a habit of gliding and banking low over the water on long, outstretched wings— appearing to "shear" the tops off waves—in between stiff, rapid flaps. Cory's is a regular but uncommon visitor to Maine waters in the summer and early fall, a long-range visitor from nesting colonies in the eastern Atlantic. About the size of a Ring-billed Gull, Cory's is our largest shearwater, separated from the more-numerous Great Shearwater by a heavy yellow bill, clean white underwings, dusky nape and neck without a "capped" look. Silent away from breeding grounds.

Brown above and white below, Cory's is fuller-bodied with broader wings than other Maine shearwaters.

Great Shearwater

Ardenna gravis

L 18" | **WS** 44"

Great Shearwater is the most common shearwater encountered in the Gulf of Maine, though its route of arrival is nothing short of remarkable. Satellite tags have revealed that the species moves from brewing grounds on the remote Tristan da Cunha islands in the southern hemisphere up along the east coast of South America, across the open Atlantic to the Gulf of Maine and Maritime provinces, before moving across to Europe and West Africa before heading south again. Can be seen offshore between June and October from whale watch boats, dedicated pelagic birding trips, or open-water ferry crossings. White neck and chin contrasts sharply with dark head, giving the bird a "capped" look.

Distinguished by sharp contrast between dark cap and white cheeks and neck, giving a "capped" look. Narrow wings with brown belly and brown patterns on the underwings also useful to separate from Cory's Shearwater.

Sooty Shearwater

Ardenna grisea

L 17" | **WS** 40"

An all-dark shearwater with whitish underwings. A long-distance migrant, visiting during the Maine summer when its southern hemisphere breeding grounds are in winter. Often seen in larger groups than other shearwaters, Sooty Shearwaters may be seen from whale watches, such as those that leave from Portland, Kennebunk, Boothbay, and Bar Harbor, as well as offshore ferry trips or dedicated pelagic birding cruises. Sooty and other shearwaters may also be seen trailing working fishing boats, hoping for an easy meal.

The only all-dark shearwater in Maine waters, showing flashes of white on underwings while flapping or banking. Slender overall, with long, thin wings.

Manx Shearwater

Puffinus puffinus

L 13" | **WS** 31"

A small shearwater, dark gray above and white below. Reminiscent of a Great Shearwater but darker, and without the defined cap. Nests primarily on islands in the cold north Atlantic, but was confirmed as a breeder on Maine's Matinicus Rock in 2009, and has continued in small numbers annually since then at what is the only known American breeding site. Rare but regular in summer from whale watches, offshore ferry boats, or dedicated pelagic birding trips. Generally silent at sea, as with other shearwaters, but gives a series of hoarse cackles at breeding colonies.

Appears black above and white below. Flies with a series of quick, snappy wingbeats interspersed with glides low over the water.

Northern Fulmar

Fulmarus glacialis

L 18" | **WS** 42"

Stocky, gull-like seabird seen only far offshore. Plumage varies among individual birds, from smoky gray to white with light gray back, the lighter color morphs most common in Maine waters. Flies unlike gulls, with stiff wing beats and frequent glides on outstretched wings. Thick, yellow-tipped bill mounted by a large nostril, the "tubenose" shared by storm-petrels, shearwaters, and other seabirds, a feature which helps these birds smell scattered patches of plankton and other prey; smell their way back to specific breeding locations; and excrete excess salt. May be seen in deep, cold water in any season, perhaps more common in fall and winter.

Stocky, bull-headed seabird most easily separated from gulls by stiff and gliding flight style. Light morph by far the most common in the Gulf of Maine.

Northern Gannet

Morus bassanus

L 31-43" | **WS** 72"

There is perhaps no more impressive an avian sight in the Gulf of Maine than feeding Northern Gannets. Wheeling over a school of fish, these massive seabirds tuck in their six-foot wings and plunge like a javelin into the water after their prey. A flock of gannets plunge-diving together, hitting the water like a volley of arrows, is a breathtaking sight and can, with luck, be viewed from rocky promontories like Dyer Point in Cape Elizabeth, Biddeford Pool, Monhegan Island, the Schoodic Peninsula, and others. Adults are white with black wing-tips, visible from a great distance, but younger birds range from all-over brown to patchy black-and-white, depending on age. A year-round Maine resident and attempted breeder, Northern Gannets are most common July through December.

.ong bill and tail. White with extensive black vingtips, unlike gulls or other birds found in he Gulf. Flies with stiff wing beats and glides.

Double-crested Cormorant

Nannopterum auritus

L 32" | **WS** 47"

Cormorants are black waterbirds which dive for aquatic prey. Their feathers are not water repellent, so cormorants spend significant time perched out of the water preening or spreading their wings to dry. The Double-crested Cormorant arrives in spring to nesting islands all along the coast, and may be found inland on most any water body as migrants move towards the St. Lawrence River during migration. When swimming, it's body is held lower in the water than ducks, loons, or grebes, almost appearing as just a "swimming neck," with a skinny neck and orange-yellow bill held high. The beautiful namesake plumes that give this species its name only present between March and May. Flocks of migratory Double-crested Cormorants often fly in long, scraggly lines or goose-like Vs, often high overhead.

Breeding plumage glossy black with white head tufts (often short and black, or missing entirely on eastern birds), green eye and orange bare facial skin.

An expert fisher, the Double-crested Cormorant swims low in the water and dives frequently.

Immature similar to adult except for variable splotchy white or tan on the breast and neck.

Great Cormorant

Phalacrocorax carbo

L 34" | **WS** 51–63"

The Maine coast marks the southernmost edge of the global breeding range of the Great Cormorant, though numbers are declining. Down to just a few nest sites on offshore islands, much of the decline can be attributed to chick predation from a rising Bald Eagle population. Larger and thicker than Double-crested Cormorants, birds in winter along the Maine coast are more likely to be Greats visiting from more northerly breeding grounds, though never as common in winter as Double-crested is in summer. Rocky coastal points like Quoddy Head, Schoodic Point, Dyer Point in Cape Elizabeth, and similar are expected vantage points in winter. Larger and thicker than Double-crested Cormorants (which are becoming more common in winter), with telltale white flank patches visible January into May.

Breeding plumage birds show white patches along the flanks and on throat. Heavier bill and thicker neck than Double-crested, and more numerous in Maine in winter.

White belly a distinctive feature on immature birds, useful to separate from Double-crested.

American Bittern

Botaurus lentiginosus

L 24-33" | **WS** 39"

A master of camouflage, the American Bittern disappears into marsh grasses as it hunts for fish and other small prey. The species breeds at freshwater wetlands across the state, though easily overlooked and its presence at breeding sites more often betrayed by its incredible booming calls, a pumping *onk-A-choonk, onk-A-choonk*. In flight the bird's large size, overall tan coloring, dark wingtips, and long yellowish legs are helpful for identification. American Bitterns may be found at coastal wetlands during migration, where exceptional high tides may push them out of the grasses and into view.

Heavily streaked light brown, buff, and tan, with heavy body and long, thick neck. American Bitterns oven freeze with bill held aloft, attempting to blend in with surrounding tall grass.

Great Blue Heron

Ardea herodias

L 38–54" | **WS** 66–79"

One of the most recognizable birds in Maine, the largest and
heaviest heron in America. Great Blue Herons are found statewide in spring and summer at almost any good-sized water
body, including marshes, coasts, rivers, lakes, and golf course
ponds. Their dark coloration and large size quickly distinguishes Great Blue Herons from any other bird in Maine except
for Sandhill Cranes, which are more active feeders and that
never coil their necks as herons do. Great Blue Herons hunt
by wading slowly or standing motionless, waiting to ambush
all manner of prey including fish, frogs, and rodents. Small
numbers may be found along the southern coast during mild
winters, including at Scarborough Marsh. Migrants arrive
in March and nest colonially at offshore islands and inland
wetlands with large dead trees. Flies slowly and steadily on
broad wings, with neck curled and long feet trailing. Their call
is a loud, ugly croak.

In flight note massive wings
tipped with dark blue, curled
neck, and long trailing legs.

A stately species, with understated plumage of blues, grays, white, and light red. Massive bill yellow underneath. Often holds neck in varying degrees of an S shape. Often encountered perched motionless at the water's edge, but also commonly hunts rodents in fields.

Great Egret

Ardea alba

L 39"　|　**WS** 54"

The lithe and lovely Great Egret can easily be distinguished
from other wading birds by its combination of stark white
plumage, black legs, and bright yellow bill. (White morph of
Great Blue Heron vanishingly rare in Maine.) A summer visitor,
Great Egrets nest on Stratton Island in Saco Bay and are
common at coastal marshes all along the south coast, including
Scarborugh Marsh, Biddeford Pool, and Rachel Carson NWR.
Less numerous Downeast and rare inland, Great Egrets may
nevertheless be seen outside of the coast in late summer after
breeding is complete, and may be seen at the marshes around
Bangor, Acadia National Park, and other suitable habitats.
Generally silent away from breeding colonies, where they utter
low croaking sounds.

Large and elegant.
Combination of
white plumage and
yellow bill unique
among Maine herons.

Snowy Egret

Egretta thula

L 24" | **WS** 39"

Another bright white heron of southern and midcoast marshes, the Snowy Egret is just over half as tall as the Great Egret, with a thin black bill, yellow at its base, and yellow feet at the end of black legs. This lovely species has made a full recovery since overhunting nearly wiped them out in the late 1800s, a massacre that served as an impetus for a national conservation movement. They've expanded since then, and have been breeding in small numbers on coastal islands since the 1960s. They're relatively common in summer at marshes from Casco Bay through the south coast, including at Gilsland Farm Audubon Center in Falmouth, Scarborough Marsh, Biddeford Pool, Rachel Carson NWR, and others. Individuals and hybrid offspring of a closely related species from Eurasia, the Little Egret, are now annual at Gilsland Farm and Scarborough Marsh, and care should be used to separate these long-plumed visitors from native Snowy Egrets.

Breeding plumage bird shows shaggy crest, thin black bill with yellow between base and eye. Black legs tipped with bright yellow feet, though colors can be obscured when muddy. Young birds have lighter colored bill and less black on legs. A quicker and more active feeder than larger Great Egret.

Little Blue Heron

Egretta caerulea

L 26" | **WS** 40"

About the size of a Snowy Egret but deep blue with a purple neck and blue bill, the Little Blue Heron is uncommon in Maine, and most likely to be found at salt marshes or coastal wetlands in spring or late summer. Adult birds are distinguished from Great Blue Herons by smaller size and lack of white on plumage. Juvenile Little Blues are white, however, and resemble Snowy Egrets from a distance, but are distinguished by their thicker, black-tipped blue bill, and dull green legs. Most often seen in marshes from Casco Bay through the south coast, including Scarborough Marsh, Biddeford Pool, and Rachel Carson NWR. They are occasional breeders on offshore islands like Stratton Island in Saco Bay, the northern extent of their breeding range.

Adult with blue body, purple neck and head, thick blue and black bill.

Juvenile birds white with bicolored blue and black bill. Slightly older birds may show piebald blue/gray and white patches.

Green Heron

Butorides virescens

L 17″ | **WS** 26″

The Green Heron is a small, dark ambush hunter typically found perching patiently on vegetation at the edge of a pond or stream. An inconspicuous and well-camouflaged species, often only noticed after flushing off its perch with a barking quok! Fairly common but easily overlooked summer resident in Maine, breeding along freshwater and brackish marshes up the coast to Mount Desert Island north to the marshes around Bangor. Dark in flight, often said to resemble a crow, with yellow feet trailing behind its tail.

Adult is a lovely blue-green with maroon neck and dark cap, dark bill and yellow legs. Can extend neck and shaggy crest when feeding or alarmed. Most often encountered perched on vegetation overhanging the water's edge, preparing to strike a variety of aquatic prey. Juvenile duller, with spotted wings and striped neck.

Black-crowned Night-Heron

Nycticorax nycticorax

L 24" | **WS** 46"

A stocky, inconspicuous, and somewhat ghostly heron, the
Black-crowned Night-Heron emerges at dusk to hunt in
shallow water along ponds and streams. Formerly common in
Maine, this species is declining due to pollution and wetland
loss, but still breeds on a handful of islands off the southern
coast. May be found in migration roosting along in dense trees
or shrubs close to water, and are regularly seen at the ponds
behind Evergreen Cemetery in Portland, around Scarborough
Marsh, Biddeford Pool, Rachel Carson NWR, and various water
bodies in northern Aroostook County. In flight utters a light,
barking, crow-like *qwock*!

Adult is chunky and hunched, with short legs, gray body,
black cap and wings, short black bill and thin white
head plumes. Pale and broad-winged in flight, may be
seen at dusk moving between roosting and feeding
areas. Immature birds are brown and speckled with thick
spots, and show thick bill with yellow lower half.

Glossy Ibis

Plegadis falcinellus

L 23" | **WS** 36"

Flocks of these dark, curve-billed waders are increasingly common in coastal marshes along the southern coast, having crossed the Atlantic from Africa in the 19th century and expanded up the Atlantic coast since then. The species has bred in Maine only since the 1970s, and is now a regular breeder on Stratton Island in Saco Bay mixed among the herons and egrets. Scarborough Marsh is the easiest place to see these birds, but other coastal and sometimes freshwater marshes between Phippsburg and Ogunquit may hold them, including Rachel Carson NWR, Biddeford Pool, Spurwink Marsh in Cape Elizabeth, Evergreen Cemetery in Portland, Gilsland Farm Audubon Center, and the Popham Beach area.

handsome bird when seen in the right light, which uminates the species' all-dark plumage into an idescent rainbow of greens, reds, and purples. ong, decurved bill is unique among Maine waders. lue facial skin and thin white line in front of dark ye. Juvenile duller with streaky head and neck In ght note broad wings, long skinny neck and small ead, trailing legs. Birds alternate between rapid ing beats and periods of gliding.

Osprey
Pandion haliaetus

L 22" | **WS** 59-71"

The Osprey is an impressive raptor found on all continents except Antarctica. They are summer visitors to Maine, arriving in early April to nest on mostly man-made structures: utility poles, channel buoys, cell towers, or especially-built nest platforms. Diet is primarily fish, caught after awe-inspiring, talon-first plunges into water. Lifting out of the water with powerful beats, Osprey arrange prey to face forward, reducing drag while flying to an elevated perch to devour. Most common on the coast and along large rivers, but may be found near lakes anywhere in the state, a major increase in numbers from a generation ago when DDT contamination caused widespread declines. Calls are a series of sharp, whistled peeps.

Large, with brown body, white neck and head with brown mask. Long, hooked bill, large talons.

Ospreys have recovered from their nadir in the mid-20th century and are once again common along waterways throughout the state.

White body, brown and white underwings showing brown "elbows" and long primary "fingers." Long wings crooked at the elbows and often held at a slight droop.

Turkey Vulture

Cathartes aura

L 28" | **WS** 69"

Turkey Vultures are now a familiar sight across Maine, having rapidly expanded its range since the late 1970s. Famous for their pink heads (a lack of feathers means less mess when sticking heads into carrion) and their soaring flight, Turkey Vultures scour the state using their excellent senses of sight and smell to locate roadkill and other carrion. Common and conspicuous in Maine from late March to early November in a variety of habitats, but perhaps most easily seen along highways or soaring on thermals near mountains and ridges. Virtually silent away from the nest. Birders should keep an eye out for another vulture species, the short-tailed Black Vulture, which is slowly but surely expanding its range into Maine.

Bare, red. head distinctive.

A huge bird with two-toned silver and black underwings. Rarely seen flapping, instead soars on outstretched wings, often gently rocking back and forth with wings slightly lifted, in a "dihedral."

Black Vulture (*Coragyps atratus*) very rare but increasing in Maine. In comparison to Turkey Vulture note broader wings, silver wing tips, black head, and relatively frequent "triple-flap" wingbeats.

Sharp-shinned Hawk

Accipiter striatus

L 10" | **WS** 17-27"

Accipiters are a group of agile, bird-hunting hawks built to move quickly and easily through dense woodland. The Sharp-shinned Hawk is our smallest, a dove-sized menace to backyard bird feeders and hedgerows. An increasing winter resident, especially along the coast, Sharp-shinned Hawks also breed throughout the state, though less commonly in southern Maine. Perhaps most evident during spring and fall migration, where it may be easily seen in large numbers from Bradbury Mountain, Mount Agamenticus, and Cadillac Mountain. Differentiating Sharp-shinned Hawks from the similar but larger Cooper's Hawk is one of the eternal challenges of birding. Look with care, and humility, for comparatively rounder head, less "capped" appearance, skinny legs and, in flight, for smaller head set deeper into forward-pushed wings. Usually silent, but near nest utters a plaintive, high-pitched *kew kew kew kew*.

Adult has small rounded head, gray back, and barred orange chest and belly. Note dark coloration extending from the head down the nape of the neck. At rest, end of tail appears square, though can be difficult to see well.

Immature birds brown with heavy brown streaking below. In flight note how head seems to set inside wings, which push forward (though not always as much as the posture in this image).

Cooper's Hawk

Accipiter cooperii

L 17″ | **WS** 25-36″

The robust and powerful Cooper's Hawk is a plus-sized version of the Sharp-shinned Hawk, with the same overall appearance, habits, and habitat. Crow-sized, the Cooper's Hawk uses stealth and speed to ambush birds at feeders, in woodlands, and even in cities. May been seen in migration from the same hawk-watches as Sharp-shinned Hawks, though are less numerous. Numbers are on the rise again after declining in the mid-20th Century due to DDT, hunting, and habitat loss, Cooper's Hawks are most common in southern Maine and remain rare further north. To separate "Coops" from "Sharpies," look for the former's larger, blockier head, which combines with a pale nape to give a capped appearance. Cooper's Hawks emit a wood-pecker-like *cak-cak-cak-ing* in defense of their nests, but are otherwise generally silent.

Adult is blue-gray above with a rusty chest and relatively thicker legs. Pale nape gives a capped look to flattish head.

Immature birds less streaked below than Sharp-shinned, with relatively larger head sticking out past the wings.

Northern Goshawk

Accipiter gentilis

L 20-26" | **WS** 40-46"

A legendarily fierce raptor of mature woodlands across the state, the Northern Goshawk is the largest of Maine's bird-hunting Accipiter hawks. Rarely encountered due to its preference for deep woods and its retiring nature, Northern Goshawks are most obvious when a hiker stumbles into a pair's territory during nesting season, when the birds are transformed into ferocious defenders. Goshawks scream at and dive-bomb interlopers, a terrifying and unforgettable experience from such a powerful bird. Rare but regular in migration from hawk-watches around the state, but many adult birds remain near nests sites through the winter. Adult defending nest gives an unmissable series of *kye kye kye* calls.

Adult is gray-blue on the back with fine gray barring on the chest and prominent white stripe above eye. Juvenile birds heavily streaked brown, with same eye stripe.

Northern Harrier

Circus hudsonius

L 19" | **WS** 43"

Unlike any other raptor in Maine, Northern Harriers act — and look — like a cross between owls and hawks. Flying low over marshes and grasslands on long, thin wings, harriers watch and listen for small mammals moving below. While a regular visitor in appropriate habitat across the state, including southern salt marshes, eastern heaths, and northern agricultural fields, harriers are rare breeders. Perches low, often on the ground, unlike other hawks in Maine. May also be seen during migration flying high past hawk watches such as Bradbury Mountain or Mount Agamenticus. Hunting style and long wings and tail are useful for identification, as is the white rump shown in all plumages. Gives a rapid series of alarmed-sounding notes when agitated.

Adult male, the "Gray Ghost," with white rump, long thin wings. Wings held in a shallow V while hunting low in banking, floaty flight.

Females larger than males, with brown plumage, heavily spotted below and heavily barred underwings. Juvenile also brown but lacks spotting on body.

Bald Eagle

Haliaeetus leucocephalus

L 28–38" | **WS** 80"

In 1969, Maine Audubon's inaugural Bald Eagle Cruise up the Kennebec River saw just a single nest. On the 50th anniversary of the cruise in 2018, passengers spotted 47 individual eagles on the same stretch of river. Such is the remarkable success of our national emblem, so decimated in the first half of the 20th century from the effects of the pesticide DDT, habitat loss, pollution, and other sources. Today the state supports well over 800 breeding pairs of these majestic raptors. An opportunistic feeder, Bald Eagles scavenges, steals, and captures a wide variety of food items including fish, small mammals, young birds, and carrion. The eagle's recovery is so thorough in Maine that its predation is now impacting other species, most notably coastal nesting populations of Great Cormorant and Great Blue Heron. Present in Maine year-round, Bald Eagles shift towards coast or other open water in winter. Though often portrayed in popular media as emitting a mighty scream (usually actually the call of a Red-tailed Hawk), a Bald Eagles call is a high-pitched, gull-like chuckle.

Bald Eagles take up to five years to reach adult plumage, and in the interim show various stages of mottled, messy brown and white. In flight, best to look for large wings held straight out to the sides.

Clean white head and tail of adult in flight is distinctive.

Adult is large, with famous white head and tail, brown body, and bright yellow bill, eyes, and feet. Often found perched high in a tree overlooking water.

Red-shouldered Hawk

Buteo lineatus

L 20" | **WS** 40"

Buteos are a genus of sturdy broad-winged hawks, most often seen soaring on thermals or watching silently from a perch waiting to pounce down on a small mammal or other prey. Red-shouldered Hawks nest in deciduous woods, near water or swamps, and often close to civilization. Their calls often give them away; a vocal species known for their clear, descending *keer, keer, keer* screeches. Blue Jays are known to mimic Red-shouldered Hawk calls, however, so beware. The species has declined in Maine over the past century, and is now largely confined to central and southern Maine. Red-shouldereds are most evident in spring, seen most regularly from the hawk-watch at Bradbury Mountain in late March into early April.

Adult with rich orange barring across chest and belly. Orange bleeds onto the shoulders where it meets boldly checkered black and white. Adult in flight shows pale crescent near wing tips and strongly barred black-and-white tail. Immature is brown above and with clean streaking below down chest and through belly. In flight shows characteristic pale wing crescents near wing tips.

Broad-winged Hawk

Buteo platypterus

L 15″ | **WS** 35″

This small buteo is a common forest breeder all throughout the state, though inconspicuous. Broad-wings are most noticeable in spring and fall migration when they come in large numbers from Central America. Often the most numerous species seen at hawk watches like Bradbury Mountain, Mount Agamenticus, or Cadillac Mountain in Acadia National Park, most numerous in fall. Broad-winged Hawks are social in migration, often forming soaring "kettles" of dozens of individuals. Birds nest in deciduous and mixed forests across Maine, where they may go unnoticed if not for their simple, plaintive high-pitched whistle: *pee-eeeeee*! Most often seen in flight, where their thickly barred tail, white underwings outlined in dark, and candle-flame-shaped wings are useful for identification.

Adult in flight shows pale underwings, with a dark trailing edge and dark wingtips. Tail is boldly patterned with thick black and white bullseye stripes.

Immature show variable amount of brown streaking below, often leaving a white spot in the middle of the breast. Tail is finely barred.

Red-tailed Hawk

Buteo jamaicensis

L 22" | **WS** 49"

The Red-tailed Hawk is a common year-round resident and the "default" buteo hawk in most of Maine. Its habit of sitting on trees above mowed roadside edges means that passengers with a keen eye are sure to spot on along any stretch of I-95, especially in winter when northern migrants add to our resident ranks. Additionally, the presence of Red-tailed Hawks is often announced by the annoyed sounds of other bird species escorting hawks off their territory, most often crows but also Red-winged Blackbirds, smaller hawks, and other birds. The rust-red tail is a giveaway for most soaring adults in Maine, but juveniles have white undertails. Birds of all ages have a dark bar on the leading edge of their wings and dark "commas" toward the wing tips. Occurs in a variety of color morphs across the country, running the spectrum from pale to dark brown, but white-chested Eastern subspecies by far the most common in Maine. Call is a hoarse, descending scream perhaps most recognizable as the "Bald Eagle" sound used in movies and TV.

Adult is large and bulky, with red tail often just visible under folded wings. Back brown often irregularly spotted with lighter feathers.

Immature is brown above with streaked belly and sides but clear white chest and throat. In flight, birds of all ages show dark feathering on front edge of inner wing.

Often perches on dead limbs or other exposed spots above fields and mowed areas, such as highways.

Rough-legged Hawk

Buteo lagopus

L 20" | **WS** 53"

The Rough-legged Hawk is a winter visitor to Maine, migrating down from its breeding grounds on the Arctic tundra. Most often seen between November and early March, most often from Aroostook County or the coast from Bangor south. Frequents areas most reminiscent of its tundra home, including large agricultural fields, airports, open marshland, and similar, where their namesake feathered legs keep cold winter winds at bay. Scarborough Marsh, Weskeag Marsh, East Point Sanctuary at Biddeford Pool, and airports in Portland, Brunswick, and Bangor are all good places to search in mid-winter. Rough-legged Hawks come in a spectrum of color morphs, with light-colored birds nearly twice as common in Maine. Generally silent in winter.

Beautiful white and brown raptor, most easily recognized in flight by its conspicuous dark "wrist" patches towards the end of its long, narrow wings. Often seen hovering over open areas in search of prey, or sometimes perched on the tips of branches which look far too fragile to hold them.

Merlin

Falco columbarius

L 11" **WS** 24"

While the name is believed to have derived from the Latin merula, meaning "blackbird," and not the mythical wizard of King Arthur fame, the small falcon Merlin is nothing less than a sorcerer in flight. Flies remarkably fast, often low to the ground or below the treetops to surprise prey, mostly birds or dragonflies. Engages in aerial stoops, twisting pursuits, and "tail-chases" on the hunt, giving the Merlin a reputation for ferocity and doggedness. Afflicted by the same pesticide-linked declines that affected many of Maine's raptors in the mid-20th century, the Merlin has rebounded and is now a common breeding bird most everywhere except the southernmost counties. Most common during migration in April, September, and October, and small numbers remain through the winter, mostly along the south coast.

Female and juvenile birds brown backed with brown streaks below. Flight is fast and direct, often low.

Small, with dark blue back and streaked and spotted underparts. Often appears all-dark in imperfect light.

American Kestrel
Falco sparverius

L 10" | **WS** 22"

Falcons are not closely related to hawks but are just as fear-some, relying on speed and surprise to capture live prey. The American Kestrel is a small, brightly colored falcon of agri-cultural fields and other grassland habitats, unfortunately declining in the state as those areas are converted to housing or forest, and as pesticides have reduced their insect prey. Still a regular sight in appropriate areas, however, the attractive kestrel is often found perched on a telephone pole or wire, or, less-commonly, by using winds to hover in place over an open field to pounce on insects or small mammals. May be seen regu-larly in summer in a variety of appropriate habitats including agricultural fields, airports, marshes, grasslands and sand plains, and regularly seen during migration in late April and in fall from hawkwatches such as Bradbury Mountain, Mount Agamenticus, Cadillac Mountain, as well as Monhegan Island.

A small, colorful falco with an orange back and buffy orange underparts. Patterne head with vertical black bars on side of face.

Wings orange on female and blue on male.

Slender, pointed wings and long tail characteristic of the fast-flying falcons. Often pumps tail while perched.

Peregrine Falcon

Falco peregrinus

L 17" | **WS** 41"

The Peregrine Falcon is one of the most famous birds in the world, and deserves its reputation as a fierce and impressive raptor. Peregrines use speed and surprise to attack a wide variety of prey such as Rock Pigeons, Blue Jays, shorebirds, ducks, gulls—more than 450 total species in North America. Hunts from a perch or from a great height, sometimes tucking wings to stoop at speeds upwards of 230 miles per hour, the fastest of any animal on Earth. A true success story, Peregrines were extirpated as a breeding species in Maine due to DDT contamination, but were reintroduced to traditional nesting sites on the cliffs of Acadia National Park and elsewhere beginning in the 1980s. Nests today in more than two dozen locations along the coast and western mountains, including the Androscoggin Valley, Mt. Kineo, and bridges and other manmade structures in Portland, Bath, and Brunswick. Can regularly be seen in migration, especially in fall at Monhegan Island. Calls include a gull-like, drawn-out wail, and a harsh *kek-kek-kek-kek*.

Large blue-gray falcon, with white chest, yellow bare part and variable barring below.

Adult in flight large, streamlined, and powerful. Strongly barred, with yellow feet and masked face. Soars easily, often alternating with stiff, shallow wing beats.

Immatures brown above, heavily streaked below, prominent brown sideburns along the face.

Snowy Owl

Bubo scandiacus

L 24" | **WS** 54"

One of the world's most breathtaking species, the Snowy Owl is a rare but regular visitor in winter. Frequency fluctuates from year to year depending on the number of lemmings, the owl's favorite prey, in the Arctic. Major "flights" or "irruptions" of owls occur every three to five years, and vary from a few dozen birds to, rarely, several hundred. Birds finding their way to Maine in winter seek out habitats reminiscent of their tunda home: open beaches, airports, treeless islands, salt marshes, and similar. The most reliable spots include the airports in Portland, Bangor and Biddeford, Brunswick Sand Plain, Biddeford Pool, Cadillac Mountain in Acadia National Park, and Scarborough Marsh. Roosts most of the day on low posts or rooftops, becoming more active at dusk. Its impressive plumage and accessibility make Snowy Owls popular with photographers and other onlookers, who can safely view the species by maintaining ample distance and not attempting to provide food. Usually silent in Maine.

A large owl, though easy to overlook in snowy conditions, with yellow eyes. Younger birds show dense, black barring on body, adults rarely pure white.

Short-eared Owl

Asio flammeus

L 15" **WS** 37"

Short-eared Owls are uncommon migrants and very rare breeding birds in Maine. They hunt for small mammals over open areas, including salt marshes, grasslands, and beaches. Is most common in fall migration, between October and early December, where it may be seen early in the morning or just before dark flying low and slow in pursuit of prey. Their flight style is agile and moth-like, with abrupt drops to capture prey. Typically seen near the coast in southern Maine, favorite haunts include Scarborough Marsh, the Portland Jetport, the Popham Beach area, and Brunswick Landing.

Medium-sized and slender. Mottled browns on the back, males streaked white below, females dark buff below. Round facial discs, dark patches around yellow eyes.

Dark "wrist" stripe on underwing, buffy patch near the tips of upperwing.

Barred Owl

Strix varia

L 19" | **WS** 41"

Barred Owls can be found in almost any forested areas in Maine, from sylvan suburban neighborhoods to deep boreal forests. Though they are year-round residents and present in good numbers they are uncommonly encountered, likely due to their dense forest habitats and their nocturnal nature. Instead, their presence is often announced by their widely-imitated hooting song, a raucous *hoo hoo ho-ho, hoo hoo ho-hoooaaawww* easily remembered as sounding like "Who cooks for you? Who cooks for you all?" Occasionally heard calling during the day but typically roots quietly close to a tree trunk, emerging after dark to hunt small mammals and a wide variety of other prey.

A large, round-headed owl with dark eyes, yellow bill, horizontal barring on the breast and vertical streaking on belly.

Hunts from a perch, flies nearly silently on large, broad wings.

Northern Saw-whet Owl

Aegolius acadicus

L 8″ | **WS** 17″

The most numerous owl in Maine is also our smallest. The
Northern Saw-whet Owl is a common resident throughout the
state, breeding in a variety of wooded areas but with a preference for dense conifer forests. Though numerous it can be very
difficult to see, as its nocturnal habits, preference for roosting
in dense conifers, and small size conspire together for secrecy.
Often the best chance to locate a Northern Saw-whet Owl is to
visit a nocturnal bird banding station, which regularly catch
the birds as they migrate south in October and November, or to
listen for its continuous, repetitive tooting call emanating from
wooded areas at night between mid-February and May. Acadia
National Park, the woods around Cape Elizabeth, and the Great
Pond Mountain Wildlands in Orland are reliable spots for this
species, though they are widely and evenly distributed.

Smaller than a
robin, with
spotted brown
back, streaked
brown-and-
white chest and
belly, and
whitish face.

Great Horned Owl

Bubo virginianus

L 22" | **WS** 40-57"

The world-famous Great Horned Owl is widespread in Maine, and is our largest breeding owl. Found most regularly in tall pines near open ground such as a marsh, river or stream, cemetery, agricultural field, or other area where it may find mammals ranging in size from mouse to skunk, as well as other prey including herons, gulls, or even other owls. Though they are common they can be difficult to find, and are most often located by their deep hoots, given at night in fall and winter to attract a mate in advance of nesting in late winter and early spring. May be seen in any suitable habitat, including large cemeteries in Portland, Bangor, and other cities, and is most common closer to the coast and less common in boreal coniferous forests in the north. Call is a low *hoo HOO hoo, hoo H'HOO hoo hoo.*

Large and powerful, with feather tuft "ears," mottled brown and white body, large yellow eyes, tawny-orange face, and massive talons.

Mostly nocturnal, but occasionally hunts during the day, pursuing mostly rodents with stiff beats of their broad wings.

Fledglings covered in snowy down, and have yellow eyes compared to dark eyes in Barred Owl owlets.

Virginia Rail
Rallus limicola

L 9" | **WS** 14"

Rails are a group of secretive waterbirds, more often heard than seen as they hunt among tall reeds or grasses. The Virginia Rail arrives in late April and may be heard at dusk and dawn calling ick, ick, kid-ick, kid-ick as they establish territories in cattail-laden marshes. Breeds near the coast in southern and mid-coast Maine up through Bangor, with scattered populations up through Aroostook County. Patient birders may spot Virginia Rails at the edges of marshes like those found at Scarborough Marsh, Rachel Carson NWR, Capisic Park in Portland, Great Salt Bay Wildlife Preserve in Damariscotta, the Viles Arboretum in Augusta, Weskeag Marsh, Essex Woods in Bangor, and the northern unit of the Moosehorn National Wildlife Refuge. Most common call is a raucous series of wheezing oinks.

Small wading bird with a long red bill, gray face, rusty breast and barred black-and white flanks. Often glimpsed at the very edges of reed beds or cattails, occasionally giving prolonged looks or swimming.

Sora

Porzana carolina

L 9" | **WS** 14"

A stocky, short-billed rail, the Sora is considered a less-numerous breeder in Maine than the Virginia Rail, but occupies many of the same locales. Strides unseen through cattails, reeds, and sedges in freshwater and brackish marshes. As with most rails, heard more often than seen, announcing its presence with a high-pitched whinny, rising and falling like the sound of mice enjoying a roller coaster. Also regularly gives a high, ascending *ker-wee*. Breeds locally throughout the state except for York County and the western mountains, but more regularly seen during migration, especially at Merrymeeting Bay in fall. Note that Maine holds a hunting season for Sora and Virginia Rail between September and early November, with a bag limit of 25 (though seeing that many of either species would be a remarkable feat).

Adult is small with a black mask, small yellow bill, brown-backed with barred flanks. Short tail often cocked. Juvenile has tan breast and face with a dull yellow bill.

Common Gallinule

Gallinula galeata

L 14" | **WS** 21"

Quite rare in Maine despite its name, the Common Gallinule breeds at just a handful of known locations scattered between York and Aroostook Counties. May appear in migration at marshy ponds near the coast, including the Sanford Lagoons complex and Biddeford Pool. Breeds irregularly at cattail marshes, most reliably at Penjajawoc Marsh and Corinna Bog near Bangor and Lake Josephine in Aroostook County. Often seen swimming, duck-like, near the edges of vegetated ponds or walking on massive feet through wet reedy marshes. Makes a series of chicken-like whinnies and squawks.

Dark-bodied with white line on the flanks, visible when swimming. Red face shield is the most obvious field mark, along with white undertail feathering.

American Coot

Fulica americana

L 16" | **WS** 24"

An uncommon migrant and rare breeder, the American Coot is at home on shallow ponds and other freshwater wetlands. Spends most of its time swimming and is often assumed at first glance to be a duck, coots do not have webbed feet but rather incredible lobed toes helping it swim but also permitting it to walk. Rare in spring, American Coots nest irregularly at just a few ponds or marshes across the state. Most common during fall migration where they may be found at waterfowl stopover sites like Sabattus Pond and Merrymeeting Bay. Makes a variety of short clucks.

All dark body contrasts with white shield topped with a red bump. Dull yellow legs.

Sandhill Crane

Antigone canadensis

L 47" | **WS** 79"

One of Maine's rarest breeders, though its range is expanding in the state. The state's first nesting pair of these elegant, long-legged birds was found near Messalonskee Lake, in central Maine near Belgrade, in 2000, and the area's wetlands and surrounding fields remain the most reliable spot to find them. Since then Sandhill Cranes have been seen annually in central and north-central Maine in summer, occasionally with young. Rare in migration both spring and fall, may be seen stalking agricultural fields or flying high with long neck extended and long legs trailing behind. Call is a loud, echoing bugle.

Juvenile smaller and rustier, lacks red cap. Very large with broad wings, extended neck, long legs trailing behind.

Adult uniform gray, with variable rusty feathers on body and red cap. Unlike Great Blue Heron, Sandhill Cranes never coil their necks.

American Oystercatcher
Haematopus palliatus

L 17" | **WS** 35"

A bold and beautiful shorebird, the crow-sized American
Oystercatcher is a rare but increasing presence in Maine.
Bivalves make up most of the menu, as its name implies,
including oysters, clams, mussels, and razor clams, as well as
the occasional crab or sand worm. The first modern breeding
record of American Oystercatcher in Maine was from 1994, on
Stratton Island in Saco Bay, and the species has since expanded
to a few other offshore islands between York and Washington
Counties. The most reliable places to see American Oyster-
catchers are on tidal flats along the southern coast, including
Pine Point in Scarborough, Biddeford Pool, Hills Beach, and
Goose Rocks Beach. Call is a loud, piping *weep*.

Bold black, white, and
brown plumage combined
with bright red bill and
yellow eye unlike anything
else on the beach. In
flight note white stripe on
wing and white rump.

American Golden-Plover

Pluvialis dominica

L 10" | **WS** 22"

The bulk of the American Golden-Plover population migrates north through the Midwest, and so this species is very rare in Maine in spring. However they're more regular beginning in late August, when nonbreeding birds begin to trickle south. More likely than Black-bellied Plover to appear inland at agricultural fields and turf farms, American Golden-Plovers are still most common along the coast, including Biddeford Pool, Scarborough Marsh, Popham Beach, and offshore islands like Monhegan. American Golden-Plovers are often found in fall in mixed flocks with the similar Black-bellied Plovers, but can be distinguished by overall brighter and more heavily patterned plumage and bold white stripe over the eye. Flight song is a high-pitched, incessant *kwe-wedl*!

Nondescript in fall nonbreeding plumage, but brighter and with smaller spotting on the back. Note white eyebrow and, in flight, lack of black "armpits" on plain gray underwings. Thinner than Black-bellied Plover, with smaller head and bill.

Black-bellied Plover

Pluvialis squatarola

L 11" | **WS** 24"

Black-bellied Plovers are most numerous and obvious in spring, between April and early June, as they prepare to move north to breeding grounds in the Arctic. In that season they may be found along any coastal flat, especially southern beaches between Wells and Falmouth, the Popham Beach area, outer Penobscot Bay and Mount Desert Island, outer islands like Monhegan and Metinic, east to Lubec. Southbound migrants begin leaving the arctic and appear back in Maine as early as July, with numbers building through the fall and some individuals remaining into late winter. Look for them hunting-and-pecking like large robins on sand beaches and mud flats. Vocal, most often hear giving a piercing, rising-and-falling *pee-o-wee!*

Breeding male is rich black through the face and belly, but note white under the tale.

Breeding female shows less black on the front. Both sexes in all plumage show telltale black "armpits," an incredibly useful field mark separating them from all other shorebirds in flight.

Nonbreeding plumage drab and yellowish, with smudgy breast. Juvenile similar but shows more extensive coloration along breast and belly.

Killdeer

Charadrius vociferus

L 9" | **WS** 18"

This bold and familiar plover is commonly found inland on open ground not necessarily close to water. Nests in a variety of open areas including dirt parking lots, ballfields, gravel roofs, airports, and other areas. A tall and active plover, the Killdeer is distinguished by its double breast band and, in flight, by its orange tail. Common in Maine from March through early winter, occasionally lingering along the coasts. The species is famous for its nest defense strategy in which it feigns a broken wing, hoping to lead a potential threat away from the nest. Call is a loud *kill-dee, kill-dee,* from which the species derives its name.

Robin-sized plover with a pair of black bands on chest, and another across forehead. Long tail.

May engage in dramatic displays to lure threats away from the nest or young, including showing off reddish rump.

Semipalmated Plover

Charadrius semipalmatus

L 7" | **WS** 15"

Named for the partial webbing between their toes, Semipalmated Plovers are common in spring and fall as they move
between northern breeding grounds and wintering areas along
the southern coasts. Seen in mudflats and on beaches almost
anywhere along the coast, though less common east of Mount
Desert Island, Semipalmated Plovers are also occasional at
inland marshes and lakes, like Taylor Bait Farm in Orono,
Sabattus Pond, or other stopover sites with muddy shorelines.
Separated from other plovers by a single breast band and
brown back. Call is an emphatic, squeaking *chu-WEET*.

Small with brown back and a single black band around
the chest, orange legs, and a short dark-tipped orange
bill. Conspicuous white wing stripe, frequently vocalizes
in flight.

Juveniles seen during fall migration, lighter brown with
a brown breast band.

Piping Plover
Charadrius melodus

L 7" | **WS** 15"

The population of this shorebird had declined to about 10 pairs in the entire state in the early 1980s, due to disturbance and predations of their nests on sandy beaches. The species was listed as Federally Threatened on the Atlantic Coast and a state endangered species, and extensive management and protections from Maine Audubon, state and federal agencies, municipalities, and hundreds of volunteers has increased that number ten-fold in the decades since. Still one of the rarest and most at-risk species in the state, Piping Plovers may be found nesting along dune edges or wrack along sandy beaches from Popham to Wells. They're masters of camouflage and can be easily overlooked; their gray backs are the color of beach sand and black neck band and forehead perfectly matches dried seaweed. Arrives in mid-March, chicks hatch in early June, and migrants depart in September. The "piping" name alludes to the bird's plaintive peeping *pee-lo* call.

Small shorebird the color of dry sand, with black forehead and narrow breast band often unconnected around breast.

Nests in small depressions in the sand, often just above the high water mark among dunes, or dried-seaweed wrack. Piping Plovers are the subjects of intensive conservation efforts in Maine.

Nonbreeding plumage rare in Maine, but sand-colored with orange legs and black bill.

Greater Yellowlegs

Tringa melanoleuca

L 12" | **WS** 24"

One of a pair of tall, speckled black-and-white shorebirds common in shallow water marshes, mudflats, and inland wetlands in spring and fall. Their namesake blonde limbs make both Greater and Lesser Yellowlegs relatively easy to distinguish from other shorebirds, but separating Greater from Lesser is a time-honored birding challenge. Both of these sandpipers actively forage for fish in shallow water, often pumping their necks as they walk. Greater is common along the coast beginning in April as the birds move towards tundra breeding grounds, and southbound birds begin arriving back in Maine as soon as July, meaning there's only a scant few weeks in the summer where Greater Yellowlegs are unlikely. Best distinguished from Lesser by longer bill, slightly upturned, and by voice, which is most commonly a strident *tew-tew-tew*, typically in groups of 3-4 syllable phrases as compared to one or two syllable phrases of Lesser (as in, Greater has a greater number of syllables, and Lesser has lesser).

Large, with solid-looking bright yellow legs. Relatively thick, slightly upturned bill is noticeably longer than the width of the head.

In flight notice white upper tail and trailing yellow legs. Both yellowlegs species often call when taking flight.

Lesser Yellowlegs

Tringa flavipes

L 9"   **WS** 24"

Another common migrant, the Lesser Yellowlegs is a near
mirror image of the Greater Yellowlegs, but with everything
just a bit smaller. Relatively common in spring, especially at
coastal marshes and tidal flats between Wells and Popham
Beach, numbers increase in fall as southbound birds may
be seen in suitable habitat all along the coast and at inland
marshes and marshy ponds. Best distinguished from Greater
Yellowlegs, with care and humility, by comparatively shorter
bill (about the same length as the head), by overall more delicate proportions, and by comparatively soft, single or doubled
too or *too-too* call.

Comparatively slender and delicate, with
slim bill only slightly longer than the
width of the head. Juveniles of both
yellowlegs species with brighter, more
contrasting spotting on back.

Solitary Sandpiper
Tringa solitaria

L 8" | **WS** 17"

A close relative of the yellowlegs but without the yellow legs, Solitary Sandpipers favor freshwater, and are common during migration at the muddy edge of ponds, wet fields, and other shallow-water habitats. They may be found beginning in late April through May at small ponds or lakes almost anywhere in Maine, and numbers pick up again in July as migrants trickle southward through September. A nondescript and easily-over-looked species, Solitary Sandpipers teeter and bounce when foraging, and, when flushed, fly with quick, flickering wing-beats and a piercing *peet-WEET*! Is not known to nest in Maine, but is the only North American shorebird to nest in trees.

Small and dark, with fine spots on the back and a white eyering useful for distinguishing from the oft-confused Spotted Sandpiper. Dark underwings and dark-centered tail.

Spotted Sandpiper

Actitis macularius

L 8" | **WS** 15"

The Spotted Sandpiper are common migrants and breeders in Maine, arriving in May and staying into October. They are rarely seen far from the edge of a water body, whether it be an inland pond or lakeshore, tidal salt marsh riverbanks, or rocky coastal islands. They nest in dirt or gravel areas like sandbars or field edges but in migration may be seen beside the water almost anywhere, including small ponds in suburban parks or along beaches. Spotted Sandpipers move with a funky gait, bobbing their bodies and dipping their backsides as they chase insects. When flushed from the shore they oven fly low over the water with rapid, flicking wingbeats followed by glide and emit a sharp *pee-weet, pee weet*.

Breeding plumage has light brown above and white below with clear brown spots. Orange bill and black and white lines on head obvious from a distance.

Nonbreeding adults and juvenile birds, late July into fall, lose breast spots and are uniform brown above with smudgy sides of chest. Walks with characteristic dipping, bopping gait.

Upland Sandpiper

Bartramia longicauda

L 12" | **WS** 26"

A large and rare sandpiper, restricted to open, grassy fields. Blueberry barrens in Downeast Maine provide essential breeding habitat, and Washington County is the species' stronghold in the state. The bird is rare elsewhere except for Kennebunk Plains in York County and near the Brunswick Airport. An unusually-proportioned shorebird, "Uppies" have long legs, a long neck and a small, dove-like head. They wade inconspicuously through tall grass and are most evident when males perch on fence posts or other prominent perches and flies up to make make spiraling display flights, accompanied by an unusual, clear, bubbling song that begins with a short trill, rises, and then falls in a drawn-out note: *who-whiip--hu-EEEEwwww*.

Tall shorebird with long neck and small head, "v" shaped chevrons down breast. Yellow bill and legs. Open seen sitting on fence post or similar perch.

Willet
Tringa semipalmata

L 15" | **WS** 28"

The Willet is a large stocky shorebird most easily separated
from its relatives in the genus Tringa by the bold black and
white patterning on wings in flight. Strictly coastal, the Willet
is a fairly common and quite vocal breeder at salt marshes
along the coast, concentrated in southern Maine. A summer
visit to Eastern Trail at Scarborough Marsh is sure to find this
species, as well as marshes in the Rachel Carson NWR, Biddeford Pool, Popham Beach and Reid State Park, and Weskeag
Marsh. Nesting birds are from the darker, heavily patterned
eastern subspecies, while fall migrants (after July) are likely to
be from the slightly larger and paler gray western subspecies.
Song is a loud, rolling, repeated *pill-will-WILLIT* given in flight.

Large and heavy, with thick legs and bill. Densely
patterned above and below in summer.

Young birds and nonbreeding adults gray and less
patterned. Fall migrants from the Western
population are light gray and lankier. Bold black
and white patterning on wings a hallmark.

Whimbrel
Numenius phaeopus

L 17" | **WS** 33"

The Whimbrel stands out among Maine's sandpipers with its large size and long, decurved bill. An uncommon migrant, especially in spring, as the birds move between breeding grounds along the Hudson Bay or Alaska. Numbers pick up beginning in July, and Whimbrel are fairly common migrants along the coast into October, most often seen on offshore islands, blueberry barrens in Washington County, and coastal shorebird hotspots including Biddeford Pool, Scarborough Marsh, the Popham Beach area, Lubec Sand Bar, and Acadia National Park. Call is a series of 6-8 sharp peeping notes given on the same pitch.

A large, stocky shorebird, easily distinguished by its long, dark, decurved bill. Large and plain brown in flight.

Ruddy Turnstone

Arenaria interpres

L 9" | **WS** 21"

A squat Ruddy Turnstone is a distinctive shorebird found along beaches and rocky coastlines. Named for its habit of flipping stones, shells, and other beachy bits in search of food, small flocks of Ruddy Turnstones arrive in spring as they make their way to breeding grounds in the arctic. Late northbound migrants mix with early southbound migrants, resulting in turnstones along our shores pretty constantly between April and November. A few birds regularly overwinter, most reliably at Biddeford Pool. In spring and when numbers peak in August they may be found at many places along the entire coast from Fort Foster in Kittery to the Lubec Flats, as well as offshore islands, but rarely inland. Their usual dipping black patch on the sides of their breast useful for separating from all other shorebirds, even in relatively drab nonbreeding plumage. A chatty species, listen for their rattling *keks* among flocks of other shorebirds.

In breeding plumage, red back and black and white markings on front unlike any other shorebird, also displayed in flight as colorful patterning.

Juveniles and adults in nonbreeding plumage have brown mottled back, but chest patterning distinctive.

Purple Sandpiper

Calidris maritima

L 8" | **WS** 17"

Unusual in being one of the few shorebirds only present in
Maine in the winter, the Purple Sandpiper is a hearty denizen
of rocky peninsulas and stone jetties. Flocks gather right at
the water's edge to forage among the barnacles. Their remote
terrain and dark coloration make them difficult to spot, and
indeed their presence is only given away when they fly to avoid
a crashing wave. Most frequently seen between October and
May, good places to look for this tenacious species includes
Dyer Point and Two Lights State Park in Cape Elizabeth,
Biddeford Pool, Pemaquid Point, the Rockland Harbor Break-
water, Schoodic Point in Acadia National Park, and many rocky
offshore islands. Dress warmly.

Dark-colored, with orange legs and
orange at the base of the bill. Flocks
of several dozen forage together on
wave-washed rocks, often only
flying to avoid being soaked.

Sanderling

Calidris alba

L 8" | **WS** 15"

Sanderling are for many a quintessential sandpiper, found on sandy beaches running up away from a gentle wave and then chasing the receding water back down. While fairly common along southern beaches in spring, before making their way to breeding grounds in the high Arctic, Sanderling are most commonly seen in late summer and fall when they can gather in flocks of several hundred on favored sites like Popham and Seawall beaches, Wells Beach, Scarborough Beach, and the Lubec Flats. Overwintering flocks not uncommon in southern Maine. Common call in flight is a set of squeaky *wick* notes.

Nonbreeding plumage is very pale gray, with a helpful black curve at the shoulder, and black legs.

Breeding plumage only briefly seen in Maine, during spring. Rich rusty above, spackled black and white. Conspicuous white wing stripe in flight.

Semipalmated Sandpiper

Calidris pusilla

L 6" | **WS** 12"

Semipalmated Sandpipers are abundant on coastal mudflats during migration, often forming large mixed flocks with other shorebirds. Named for the partial webbing between their toes, Semipalmated Sandpipers are common in spring but abundant in late summer after they leave their tundra breeding grounds. Flocks of hundreds or thousands swarm over mudflats, moving ahead while probing the mud for invertebrates. Identification of Semipalmated Sandpiper in late summer can be very tricky as molting adults mix with juvenile birds (and other species, especially Least Sandpiper). "Semipalms" are comparatively larger and duller than Leasts, and have black legs instead of yellow. Call is a short, high-pitched squeaky *chip* or *chirp*.

Back color on adult variable from grayish-brown to dull rufous, with black spotting above, arrow-shaped markings across the sides of the chest and breast, and dark legs.

Juveniles show crisp plumage in fall, with light edges to new feathers creating a scalloped and scaly effect. Dark olive legs in all plumages.

Least Sandpiper

Calidris minutilla

L 6" | **WS** 11"

The Least Sandpiper small, abundant, and widespread in Maine in spring and from late summer into October. Its greenish yellow legs are a helpful field mark, but beware they can often be covered in mud. More common inland than others of the "peep" sandpipers, Leasts may be found in ponds and wetlands throughout the state during migration but are always most common along the coast where they join mixed flocks of other shorebirds to feed on exposed mud, often near grass or debris. Numbers peak when southbound migrants and newly-fledged young refuel at coastal sites anywhere between the Lubec Flats in Washington County to Fort Foster in Kittery, across the river from New Hampshire. Walks slowly, often sweeping its bill side to side as it probes. Call is a slightly drawn-out *treat*.

Dark brown to reddish brown above, with prominent black with prominent dusky streaking across breast, a slender, fine-tipped bill, and yellowish legs. Juveniles brighter rufous.

Nonbreeding birds, later in fall, brownish with telltale dull yellow legs. Thin bill with a fine tip. A Thin white wing stripe evident in flight.

Pectoral Sandpiper

Calidris melanotos

L 9" | **WS** 17"

A medium-sized sandpiper, often said to resemble a large
Least Sandpiper, the Pectoral Sandpiper is easily overlooked
in grassy salt marshes or flooded fields. An uncommon spring
migrant between late March and early June, numbers pick up
as birds depart their breeding grounds, and "Pecs" can sometimes be found in flocks of several dozen at favored sites such
as Scarborough Marsh, Sabattus Pond, Cobbosseecontee Lake,
Sebasticook Lake, as well as turf farms, grassy mudflats, and
saltmarshes anywhere else in the state. The Pectoral Sandpiper
is brown and bulky, and easily identified by the fine streaking
on its breast which stops abruptly at its white belly. The flight
call is a rapidly-trilled *triiiip*.

A bulky brown sandpiper with dull green legs
and fine streaking on breast which stops abruptly
at the breast. Less pronounced in nonbreeding
plumage but still the most evident field mark.

Baird's Sandpiper

Calidris bairdii

L 7.5" | **WS** 17"

A rare migrant sandpiper found typically along the coast in fall. The majority of Baird's Sandpipers migrate north to the tundra in Alaska and Canada via the American Midwest and West, and there are no spring records in Maine. Typically 20-30 individuals are seen each fall in Maine on their southbound migration, usually juvenile birds. There are a handful of inland records, but birds are most often seen along the coast, especially at Seawall and Popham beaches, Scarborough Marsh, Biddeford Pool, and the Laudholm Farm area in Wells. Identification can be tricky, but note the long wings extending past the tail, and small pale dot between bill and eye.

ong wings give Baird's Sandpipers
 elongated look. Black legs and
 aly upperparts on juvenile, with
 nall white spot between bill and eye.

White-rumped Sandpiper

Calidris fuscicollis

L 7" | **WS** 17"

Slightly larger than the classic "peep" sandpipers—Semipal-mated and Least Sandpipers, in Maine—the White-rumped Sandpiper can be found with patience in mixed species shore-bird flocks in spring and fall. The species is famous for its long migrations, migrating between the Arctic tundra and southern South America each year on long, pointed wings which extend past the tail and give the bird an elongated profile. With a few exceptions (Sanford Lagoons, Sabattus Ponds, Aroostook County, Sebasticook Lake), the White-rumped Sandpiper is a coastal visitor, mixing in with flocks of other sandpipers on mudflats anywhere on the coast, more often south, from late July to early November. Call is a high-pitched, mousy squeak.

Fairly nondescript, with a grayish brown back, long wingtips, crisp breast streaking, white eyestripe, and a slightly drooping bill. White rump only visible in flight, and may help pick this species out of a mixed flock of flying shorebirds.

Dunlin
Calidris alpina

L 7" | **WS** 15"

A long-billed sandpiper of sandy beaches and mudflats, though also found inland during fall migration along lakeshores and other shorebird stopover sites. Dunlin are fairly common in spring along Maine's southern coast, at hotspots including Scarborough Marsh, Biddeford Pool, and the Popham Beach area, where they are easily separated from other shorebirds by their combination of long bill and black belly. Southbound migrants return in August, later than other species, and peak from late September into late November, at inland stopover sites like Sabattus Pond or Sebasticook Lake, or, more commonly, along the coast. A small number of Dunlin spend the winter in Maine, typically at Biddeford Pool, Popham Beach, or sandy beaches along the southern coast, where they often mix with Sanderling. These fall and winter birds lack the black belly, and are characterized by their overall gray color, and long drooping bill. The call note is a scratchy *djeeep* given in flight.

No other shorebird in spring has combination of black belly and long, black, drooping bill. Rusty red on back and cap.

Non-breeding plumage is grayish brown on the back and head. Black legs and long, black, drooping bill.

Red Knot

Calidris canutus

L 10" | **WS** 21"

The Red Knot in its salmon-red breeding plumage is a sight to behold, though one becoming rarer. The species has declined more than 80% in previous decades, due in large part to habitat loss and the reduction of its favorite food, horseshoe crab eggs, along its migratory route. Red Knots are currently listed as Threatened under the Endangered Species Act, and Maine migrants may spot colorful leg bands from researchers, which can be reported back to help track their movements. Spring breeding-plumage birds are uncommon in Maine, but numbers pick up slightly beginning in July as birds return from the Arctic. Late-summer birds in molt show remnants of reddish on the belly, and nonbreeding birds are a nondescript gray.

A chunky sandpiper with salmon-red belly, chest, and face, and red and gray checkered back.

Juveniles and nonbreeding adults are gray, with streaking or slight barring down the sides, and dull yellow or olive legs, and a stout black bill.

Short-billed Dowitcher

Limnodromus griseus

L 11" | **WS** 19"

If placed side-by-side with the Long-billed Dowitcher, North America's other dowitcher species, the Short-billed Dowitcher would indeed have the shorter appendage. But not by much, and, confusingly, the Short-billed Dowitcher has a comparatively longer bill than most any shorebird its size. Don't focus on bill length, is what I'm saying, and instead focus on the reddish color on spring and early fall migrant birds, the darkly barred flanks on nonbreeding birds, and the sewing machine-like probing motion in feeding birds of any age. Fairly uncommon in Maine in spring, most often in southern Maine, Short-billed Dowitcher numbers pick up in early July and peak in late summer. Sound in many coastal shorebird hotspots like Scarborough Marsh, Pine Point in Scarborough, Popham Beach, and Biddeford Pool. Call is a *rapid tu-tu-tu*, most often given in flight.

Medium-sized with long bill, stripes on head, and a rusty breast and sides, dotted with spots, fading to whitish on belly. Juveniles are buff- or rust-breasted, with red and black feathering on back. Note spotted flanks.

Wilson's Snipe

Gallinago delicata

L 12" | **WS** 17"

A well-camouflaged denizen of wet fields or the vegetated margins of freshwater ponds, Wilson's Snipe nest throughout the state, more commonly in the east and north. Their breeding displays are unforgettable, males fly high in the air above bogs, marshes, or other wetlands, and produce an eerie winnowing sound from the air passing over modified tail feathers. Outside of breeding areas they can be common during migration in late March and April, and then in late summer through fall, particularly at favorite marshes like Scarborough or Weskeag but in any similar habitat. Finding snipe can be a challenge, though, as they can hide low in vegetation and don't flush easily. Such is the difficulty in finding them that they are a popular game bird, with Maine holding a season for them between September and mid-December. When flushed they produce a raspy chirping noise in flight.

Densely patterned browns and tans above. Long bill, typically held downward, for probing deep into the mud for earthworms.

American Woodcock

Scolopax minor

L 11" | **WS** 18"

A unique and unforgettable bird, the American Woodcock is a widespread and common upland shorebird, though due to its secretive habits and cryptic plumage is extremely difficult to find outside of the early breeding season. Woodcock are early migrants, arriving in March and beginning their famous breeding displays in clearings and grassy fields. Males emerge at dusk and begin uttering a series of nasal *peent* notes, followed by a chirping and twittering as he flies high into the air and zig-zags back to the ground. Stays out of sight for the rest of the summer and fall, probing for earthworms in forests and fields. American Woodcock are hunted in Maine during a state-sanctioned season between October and late November.

A rotund shorebird with short legs, a big eye, and a long pinkish bill. Cryptically patterned with gray and black above and buff below. Flies on rounded wings with quick fluttering wing beats when flushed.

Red Phalarope

Phalaropus fulicarius

L 8.5" | **WS** 17"

Red Phalaropes are rare in Maine in spring and fall as they move offshore from wintering grounds in the southern Atlantic and breeding grounds on the Arctic tundra. Incredibly for such tiny birds, Red Phalaropes and their close cousins the Red-necked Phalaropes almost never come to land outside of the breeding season, and instead spend their lives on the open ocean feeding on zooplankton and other small marine invertebrates. Very rare in spring during a brief migratory window in May and June, seen deep in the Gulf of Maine. More numerous in late summer to late fall, similarly far offshore, becoming more common off the northeast coast. Often seen flying low and fast in tight flocks or resting on the water near patches of floating seaweed.

Female phalaropes are larger and more brightly colored than males in breeding plumage, though rarely seen in Maine waters.

Red-necked Phalarope

Phalaropus lobatus

L 7.75" | **WS** 15"

The Red-necked Phalarope a small pelagic shorebird seen with luck from offshore ferries, or pelagic birding or fishing trips. Similar to the Red Phalarope, the species may be found during spring migration between May and June as they work their way up to tundra breeding grounds, and headed southbound again just a few months later. The species at one time could be found in the millions in Passamaquoddy Bay in far Downeast Maine, feasting with hundreds of thousands of gulls on zooplankton stirred up by the strong tides. But a shift in food availability brought upon a rapid decline in this species in the Bay, dropping from millions to near zero between the 1970s and late 1980s.

Nonbreeding plumage much more common in Maine. Streaked gray back with dark eye spot. Red Phalarope in nonbreeding plumage shows lighter, softer, unstreaked gray on back.

Female Red-necked Phalarope in breeding plumage is a stately bird, with gray body and head, white throat patch, and deep red neck patch.

Black-legged Kittiwake
Rissa tridactyla

L 16" | **WS** 37"

A beautiful, small gull of open oceans, rarely seen from land.
Most abundant in the Gulf of Maine through fall and winter
when it returns from breeding cliffs in the Maritimes and the
northern St. Lawrence River. Best opportunities to see from
land are from offshore islands like Monhegan, from pelagic
whale watches or fishing charters, or from rocky promintaries
like Dyer Point in Cape Elizabeth, Schoodic Point, or Pemaquid
Point when late season Nor'easters blow the birds towards
shore. The largest concentrations are far Downeast, where
birds numbering in the thousands may be seen feeding on tidal
upwellings in the waters around Eastport and Campobello.
Buoyant in flight, dips and plunges into the sea like a tern in
pursuit of prey. Generally quiet away from nesting cliffs.

Small gull with plain gray back, white
tail, unmarked yellow bill, and jet
black wing tips, often referred to as
looking like the wings had been
"dipped in ink."

Immature birds have bold black M
pattern on the back, black tail tips
and black collar around neck.

Bonaparte's Gull

Chroicocephalus philadelphia

L 13" | **WS** 31"

Our smallest commonly-seen gull, with relatively thin, narrow wings and light-colored plumage. Present throughout the year, with small numbers of wintering birds found locally along the coasts before the species moves north to breeding grounds in the northern boreal forest, nesting, atypically for gulls, in conifer trees. Bonaparte's Gulls have made very rare attempts at nesting in the state, but the vast majority remain instead along the coasts, peaking in numbers in late summer anywhere where food is abundant. August numbers feeding in Passama-quoddy Bay, far Downeast, can run into the several thousands. But may be found anywhere along the coast, feeding by sitting on the water or walking on mudflats, generally not in the company of other gulls. Call is a raspy, high-pitched *keeeh*.

...mall, black-headed gull in summer, with thin black bill, pink legs, ...nd distinctive white pattern on the ends of wings. Nonbreeding ...rds lack black hood.

...nmatures show black braces on upperwing close to body, but ...ck black collar of immature Black-legged Kittiwake.

Laughing Gull

Leucophaeus atricilla

L 16" | **WS** 36–47"

A medium-sized black-hooded gull, abundant and garrulous in summer along the coast. Nests on offshore islands, including those managed for rare tern species and alcids, where Laughing Gulls are actively discouraged. May be seen anywhere along the coast in summer, though most common south of the Schoodic Peninsula and in areas closer to their nesting islands, such as the Boothbay Harbor area and Muscongus Bay. The species takes two years to reach adult plumage, going from a dusky brownish to adult plumage with its dark gray back, black wing tips, black hood with red bill, and white eye-arcs. The Laughing Gull gets its name from its incessant *ha-haa* calls.

A handsome bird in adult breeding plumage, with dark gray back, black wing tips, black hood, deep red bill and legs, and white eye-arcs.

Ring-billed Gull

Larus delawarensis

L 19" | **WS** 44"

The Ring-billed Gull is a common and widespread species in Maine, and is the most common gull found away from the coast. It's unafraid to cozy up to human civilization, and as a result is sometimes derided as a dumpster-diver. More accurate would be to call it an opportunist, a species equally at home on freshwater lakes or on the coast, in cities and agricultural fields, in shopping mall parking lots and remote rocky beaches. The majority of the species breeds in Canadian forests, but is expanding its summer range in northern Maine, and now several hundred pairs nest colonially in Aroostook County. Most numerous in fall and winter wherever the Ring-billed Gull can find open water, or a discarded french fry. Call is a shrill *eee-oww*, similar but higher pitched than the larger Herring Gull.

A medium-sized gull with a namesake black ring around a yellow bill. Black wing tips with white spots, yellow legs. Similar in winter but with some brownish streaking on head.

Takes three years to reach adult plumage, and can be relatively messy in the interim, with pink bill with dark tip, pinkish legs, and mix of gray and brown feathers (more gray the closer to adult).

Herring Gull

Larus argentatus

L 24" | **WS** 56"

Herring Gulls are the default gull along the coast, where it is common and abundant all year long. Breeds on many offshore islands as well as rooftops in downtown Portland, where visitors can't go a few minutes without seeing one of these large birds wheeling overhead or hearing their blaring calls echoing through the alleyways. Less common inland but possible on almost any body of freshwater lake, or even plowed fields. Despite their ubiquitousness, Herring Gull numbers are dropping nationally due to less-wasteful fishing practice and the closure of many open landfills. The species takes four years to reach adult plumage, and identification of sub-adults (of all gull species) can be a challenge. Vocalizations are synonymous with time spent on the Maine coast and include a drawn-out, plaintive *keow* and a long series of laughing notes.

Adult with light gray back, black wing tips with white spots, yellow bill with orange spot, pink legs. In winter, adult head and neck are streaked with smudgy brown.

Immature birds variable, but typically brownish and spotted, with dark bill gaining pinkish color as the bird ages.

Birds in their third winter are mostly gray-backed, with stray brownish feathers, a lack of white wing spots, and the remnants of black on a pinkish or yellowish bill.

Iceland Gull

Larus glaucoides

L 22" | **WS** 49"

Iceland Gulls along with Glaucous Gulls are the two "white-winged gulls" that arrive along the Maine coast in small numbers in winter. Smaller and dantier than Herring Gulls, Iceland Gulls are easily recognized by the very limited or complete lack of black in their wingtips. Mixes freely with wintering flocks of gulls anywhere they occur in winter, including downtown wharves in towns like Portland, Rockland, Lubec, and Bar Harbor and along major rivers including the Kennebec and Penobscot. Generally silent in Maine.

Adult pale gray back, wingtips vary from all-white to spotted with black. In flight always shows less black than Herring Gull. Thin yellow bill.

Immatures range from very pale brown all over to nearly all white, with thin all-dark bill.

Glaucous Gull

Larus hyperboreus

L 27" | **WS** 60"

Another uncommon white-winged winter visitor, Glaucous Gulls may be found in many of the same places as Iceland Gulls and other wintering species, including wharves, inland land-fills, and anywhere else with a steady supply of food. Typically only younger birds are seen in Maine, as distinguished from young Icelands and other immature gulls by the large size and long, large pink bill with dark tip. May hybridize with Herring Gulls, making for a challenging identification. Generally silent in Maine.

Immature birds range from overall pale white to fawn-colored. Note lack of black in wingtips and thick bicolored bill.

Adults rare in Maine but are large with complete lack of black in wingtips. Nonbreeding winter birds show some brownish streaking on head. Yellow bill, pink legs.

Great Black-backed Gull

Larus marinus

L 30" | **WS** 60"

The King of the Coast, the Great Black-backed Gull is the
largest gull in the world. In adult plumage this species is
easy to pick out from among more numerous species, with its
graphite gray back and pink legs. This commanding species has
an attitude to match, and is regularly seen chasing and preying
upon songbirds caught out to sea and a wide variety of young
birds, among a varied diet that includes everything from shell-
fish to carrion. Nests colonially on a number of coastal islands.
Uncommon inland, unless within flying distance of a land-
fill, Great Black-backs may be found almost anywhere along
the coast. Calls lower-pitched than Herring and other gulls,
including a barked *kowp, kowp,* and a deep, winnied laugh.

Large and
commanding, with a
dark gray back, pink
legs, and yellow bill.

Immature birds large with heavy, mostly all-dark bill. Mostly whitish on head and front with black-and-white patterned back.

The Great Black-backed Gull is the largest gull species in the world. Rarely seen away from the immediate coast.

Lesser Black-backed Gull

Larus fuscus

L 23" | **WS** 56"

A rare but increasing visitor to Maine during migration and through the winter, adult Lesser Black-backed Gulls are most easily differentiated from other species by their combination of dark gray back (darker than Herring and Ring-billed Gulls) and yellow legs. Wintering birds are presumed to be from a growing population of breeding birds in Greenland. Is possible wherever gulls congregate in winter, including beaches, wharves, piers, and other congregations. Immature birds are common as well and make for a challenging identification, but are generally whiter-headed than other species as young birds, slightly smaller and more tapered than Herring Gulls.

Nonbreeding adult with gray back several shades darker than Herring or Ring-billed, with yellow leg. Species is much smaller and more slender than the darker-backed Great Black-backed Gull.

Juvenile birds dark billed and fairly cleanly checkered overall, in comparison to other gulls of similar age, with darker flight feathers than Herring Gull.

Least Tern
Sternula antillarum

L 9" | **WS** 20"

Beach-nesting birds like the tiny, yellow-billed Least Tern have had a tough time of things, displaced by human development, by beachgoers and their pets, by increasing predators like foxes and crows, and by rising seas. Least Tern numbers in Maine cratered in the early 1980s, but decades of effort have helped bring their numbers up again, and the species currently nests colonially on a handful of sandy beaches in southern Maine. Good places to look for these vocal terns after they arrive in April is the Nonesuch River (including Scarborough Marsh, Pine Point Lobster Co-Op, and Pine Point Beach), Popham and Seawall beaches in Phippsburg, and the Laudholm Farm area in Wells. Calls with a raspy *zreeek* and a squeaky two syllable *ke-DEEK*.

Robin-sized bright white tern with white forehead interrupting black cap. No other tern in Maine has a yellow bill.

Black Tern

Childonias niger

L 9" | **WS** 23"

All-dark plumage and freshwater habits separate Black Terns
from any other tern species in Maine. A rare breeder in Maine
and listed as endangered on the state endangered species list,
the species nests on just a handful of known sites, freshwater
marshes or ponds in the middle of the state. The easiest place
to see them is from the boat ramp at the south end of Messalonskee Lake between May and early August, where the birds
can be seen plucking small fish and insects off the surface
of the water. Rarely seen away from breeding colonies, but
possible nearly anywhere during migration, especially along
the coast. Calls are a high-pitched *chip* or *yip*.

Breeding plumage deep black on body, white
undertail and tail, gray underwings.

Molting birds show a messy pattern of black
and white. Nonbreeding plumage white
bodied and gray backed with black spot
behind eye.

Roseate Tern

Sterna dougallii

L 15" | **WS** 28"

Impacted first by plume hunters and now by habitat loss, predation, and climate change, the exquisite Roseate Tern is listed as endangered under both state and federal endangered species laws. It is known to breed alongside Common Terns on just a handful of offshore islands, including Stratton Island and Eastern Egg Rock. Stratton birds often feed with other terns in the lower reaches of the Nonesuch River in Scarborough, and Pine Point Beach, the Pine Point Co-Op parking lot, and Western Beach are some of the more likely places to pick out this species from shore. Similar to Common and Arctic terns, Roseate Terns are bright white, with longer tails and less black on the wings than either species. Their harsh two-syllable calls *CHI-wi* may be picked out of flocks of other species.

Very white tern with all black or mostly black bill and long tail streamers and fast, stiff wingbeats. Often seen in the company of Common Terns.

Common Tern

Sterna hirundo

L 12" | **WS** 30"

The most abundant tern in Maine and the most likely to be seen from shore, Common Terns arrive off Maine's coast in May and may be seen throughout the summer feeding in nearshore waters almost anywhere along the coast from Kittery to Lubec. They nest offshore on more than a dozen nesting islands, some with hundreds of nests, and also on a few freshwater lakes in far northern or northwestern Maine, including Long Lake in Aroostook County, and several lakes along the Allagash Wilderness Waterway. Flies on rowing wingbeats, calling incessantly, and dives into the water for small fish. Calls include a grating *kearrr* and a quick *pip-pip*!

In breeding plumage note black cap, deeply forked tail, and orange-red bill with black tip. Shows fairly extensive blackish wedge on wing tips from above and below in flight.

Adult in nonbreeding plumage with white forehead, black bar on shoulder, black bill. Juvenile birds, seen in July and August, are brownish and scalloped on back with black shoulder bar.

Arctic Tern
Sterna paradisaea

L 12" | **WS** 31"

The Arctic Tern holds the record for longest migration of any animal on Earth, a more than 40,000 mile annual round trip flight from wintering grounds off Antarctica to breeding grounds in the northern latitudes, including in the Gulf of Maine. There are fewer than ten known nesting colonies on offshore islands, including Matinicus Rock, Seal Island National Wildlife Refuge, and Stratton Island in Saco Bay. Less commonly seen from the mainland than Common Terns, with which they frequently associate offshore, Arctic Terns may be picked out with care from feeding flocks at the mouth of the Nonesuch River at Pine Point, at Popham Beach State Park, and other places where large numbers of terns congregate. Gives a shrill scream, similar but higher pitched than Common Tern.

To separate from similar Common Tern, note Arctic's deep, all-red bill, and thin line of black along the tips of wing feathers.

Parasitic Jaeger

Stercorarius parasiticus

L 17" | **WS** 46"

Jaegers are a family of seabirds related to gulls with a reputation for chaos. They are known for harassing gulls and terns over open water, chasing them until they drop their food for the jaeger to snatch up. Each of the three jaeger species are possible in the Gulf of Maine, but Parasitic Jaeger is most common, followed by Pomarine Jaeger and Long-tailed Jaeger. As pelagic species, the best chance for a Parasitic Jaeger is from a whale-watching boat or dedicated pelagic birding trip between May and September, though scattered sightings occur into December. Variable plumages and color morphs, combined with often less-than-ideal viewing conditions, make jaeger identification tricky, but look for pointed central tail feathers and relatively "neutral" proportions, with neither wings nor tail looking especially long.

Light morph adult in flight shows white belly, long, pointed tail feathers, brown cap. Jaegers are often first noticed when in relentless pursuit of a gull or tern. Other color morphs dark brown to cinnamon.

Black Guillemot

Cepphus grylle

L 13" | **WS** 21"

Among the most iconic of Maine's avifauna are our breeding populations of alcids: small, oceanic seabirds including puffins, murres, and guillemots. The Black Guillemot is the smallest of Maine's breeding alcids, and the easiest of the family to see from shore. They breed on more than 100 coastal islands from York County in the south all the way Downeast to Passama-quoddy Bay, and are easily identified in summer by the large white patches on their deep black body, and bright red feet. They molt into an overall whitish plumage in winter, though white wing patches are still evident, and may be seen swimming inconspicuously near shore, periodically diving for fish. Calls near breeding colonies with a high-pitched piping.

Breeding plumage deep, shiny black with bright white wing patches. Silver underwings and bright red feet evident in flight.

Nonbreeding birds whitish, with remnants of white wing patches evident on darker wings in flight.

Common Murre

Uria aalge

L 17" | **WS** 26"

A large and slender alcid, nesting in small numbers on a few offshore islands including Matinicus Rock and Machias Seal Island. Most reliably seen on dedicated birding trips or puffin cruises to their nesting islands, where they can be found lounging on the rocks with other seabirds or diving for fish, squid, and other marine creatures. Rarely seen in Maine waters outside of the breeding season. Can be separated from other of Maine's breeding alcids by deep chocolate brown, not black, coloration, dusky flanks, and long, pointy bill. A percentage of Maine birds from the "bridled" morph, which show an attractive white eye ring and facial line.

Large, football-shaped bird, with deep brown plumage above and white below, with barred flanks. White encroaches brown head in winter, leaving just a brown stripe down away from eye.

Thick-billed Murre

Uria lomvia

L 18" | **WS** 28"

A close relative of the Common Murre, but the Thick-billed Murre does not breed in Maine. Instead it's a rare but regular winter visitor and a treat for those willing to seek birds from rocky, ocean coasts in Maine's harshest season. Most often peninsulas such as East Point in Biddeford Pool, Dyer Point in Cape Elizabeth, Pemaquid Point, and Schoodic Point, where they may be seen diving for fish in nearshore waters. Can be separated from Common Murre in nonbreeding plumage by solid black above and white below, including chin and throat. Silent in winter.

Large seabird, black above and white below, with white on chin and throat. Thicker, stubbier bill than Common, which has more white on head in winter plumage.

Razorbill

Alca torda

L 17" | **WS** 26"

A large black-and-white alcid found in summer around a handful of offshore breeding colonies and in winter along rocky sea coasts. Along with other alcids, numbers have increased in Maine since the middle of the 20th century, when overhunting and habitat loss pushed their numbers to the brink. Now relatively stable on islands including Matinicus Rock, Seal Island, Petit Manan, and others, and the species is reachable in summer via dedicated pelagic birding trip or puffin cruise from New Harbor, Boothbay Harbor, or Bar Harbor. The most common alcid seen from coastal promontories in winter, including Schoodic Point, Pemaquid Point, Dyer Point and Two Lights State Park, East Point at Biddeford Pool, and others, as the birds dive and loaf in nearshore waters or flying low over the water with rapid wing beats. Makes low growling noises near the nest, silent in winter.

Long and solid-looking, black above and white below. Thick bill with white stripes in breeding plumage. White creeps up behind eye in nonbreeding plumage, look for combination of thick bill, long tail, and white behind head to separate from murres.

White creeps up behind eye in nonbreeding plumage, look for combination of thick bill and white behind head to separate from murres.

Dovekie

Alle alle

L 8" | **WS** 15"

Spotting a Dovekie is the rare reward for braving the winter weather along Maine's rocky coasts, as the species reaches the southern extent of their wintering range in the Gulf of Maine after breeding in Greenland and northern Europe. A tiny alcid, smaller than a robin, a lucky and patient birder may spot a Dovekie from rocky peninsulas like Nubble Point, Dyer Point and Two Lights State Park, Pemaquid Point, Schoodic Point, and others, often by arriving early to catch the small birds in flight to feeding areas; their size makes them easy to lose among the waves while on the water. May be blown close to shore or wrecked by winter storms. Silent at sea in Maine.

A tiny black-and-white football with a stubby little bill and relatively long wings. Most often picked out while flying low and landing inelegantly into the sea.

Atlantic Puffin

Fratercula arctica

L 13" | **WS** 21"

Maine's most famous bird, the gorgeous Atlantic Puffin is also a true success story. Nearly extirpated from the state by over-zealous hunters and introduced predators in the early 1900s, intensive management led by the National Audubon Society have helped bring the species back to more than 1,100 nesting pairs on at least five offshore islands. Viewing wild puffins is more difficult than finding them on a t-shirt or keychain in a coastal gift shop, and requires a dedicated boat trip from New Harbor, Boothbay Harbor, Mount Desert Island, Cherryfield, or other. The trip is worth the effort, as viewers are treated to the sight of thousands of individual puffins, murres, terns, Razorbills, gulls, and other species rarely seen anywhere else. Atlantic Puffins are easily picked out among the swirling masses, given away by the bright yellow, red, and blue bills from which they derive their nickname, the Sea Parrot. Rarely seen in nonbreeding plumage in Maine, which is muted and dusky. Voice at nesting colonies is a low drawn-out moan.

Unmistakable in breeding plumage, with large triangular bill, white cheeks with triangular skin around eye with trailing crease and black and white body.

Generally, seen in flight only between colony and feeding grounds. Flights higher off the sea surface than other alcids.

Atlantic Puffins are only rarely seen from the mainland, instead requiring a charter company to reach breeding colonies offshore.

Rock Pigeon

Columba livia

L 13" | **WS** 23"

Native to Europe, India, and North Africa, the Rock Pigeon
has been carried by humans around the globe, and it is now
one of the world's most familiar species. They are ubiquitous
in Maine wherever there is civilization, and nest under over-
passes, in barns, on buildings, and cliffs. Often disregarded by
birdwatchers, Rock Pigeons should be appreciated for their
aerial abilities, which include strong, fast, flying and aerial
acrobatics. Centuries of domestication have resulted in a host
of plumages and colors, including the natural gray-backed
morph, as well as all dark or mostly reddish brown variations,
and others. Their call is a soft and rolling cooing.

Common in a variety of colors,
including reddish brown, pied, all
dark and all light.

Large, chunky bird with gray body,
iridescent green feathering on neck,
and two black bars on wings. White
underwings and rump evident in flight.

Mourning Dove

Zenaida macroura

L 11" | **WS** 16"

One of the most common and numerous birds in the country, the Mourning Dove has expanded northward over the past century to include all of Maine except our deepest forests. Rarely found far from human civilization, especially those humans with backyard bird feeders, Mourning Doves may be found on rooftops, overhead wires, or foraging for seeds in lawns, agricultural fields, or other open ground. Bursts into flight with a twittering sound made by their wings, this species is a strong flier, sometimes mistaken for a small hawk or falcon. Sings a familiar, gentle, and melancholy cooing song, *hoo HOO hooo hooo*.

Flies fast and straight, with long pointed tail. Spreads tail on takeoff and landing, showing black and white spots on outer tail feathers.

Medium-sized, tan with blue ring around eye, black wing spots, and long, pointed tail.

Yellow-billed Cuckoo

Coccyzus americanus

L 11" | **WS** 16"

An uncommon migrant and breeder in southern Maine, the shy and reclusive Yellow-billed Cuckoo is easily overlooked as it hunts for caterpillars in the canopies of tall deciduous trees. Arrives in Maine in late May and occupies forests in the coastal counties up to about Bangor. Departs in September and early October, when visiting migratory hotspots like Monhegan Island, Biddeford Pool, or the Rachel Carson NWR may provide the best opportunities to see this species. In summer, most birds are located by their calls, a rapid, knocking series of hard barks: *ku-ku-ku-ku-ku-ku-keow-keow-keow-keowp-keowp*, typically given from high in a shaded perch in the canopy, also a rapid series of metallic knocks.

Light brown above, white below, with long tail with white spots underneath. Curved yellow bill and yellow eye ring. May sit motionless in the canopy for long periods. Wings reddish above and white below. Long, pointed wings and long tail give the bird a unique profile in flight.

Black-billed Cuckoo

Coccyzus erythropthalmus

L 12" | **WS** 15"

The Black-billed Cuckoo, like the closely related Yellow-billed Cuckoo, is an uncommon breeder in southern Maine north to Bangor, though more frequently makes appearances further north. Arrives in late May and breeds in early successional deciduous woodlands or dense thickets, where it can be difficult to spot as it sits motionless and occasionally hunts for caterpillars. Both of Maine's cuckoos have the ability to shed their stomach linings, as an owl disgorges a pellet, in order to rid themselves of troublesome caterpillar hairs. Departs in mid-September. Most often given away by its call, a smooth and soft, rapid series of coos: *coo-coo-coo, coo-coo-coo.*

Brown-backed and white below, with dark bill, gray cap, and red ring around the eye. In flight shows all brown wings, and small white tips on tail feathers unlike the large black-and-white tips on Yellow-billed Cuckoo.

Common Nighthawk

Chordeiles minor

L 9" | **WS** 22"

Nightjars are a family of birds which feed on flying insects at night. The Common Nighthawk is the most common of Maine's nightjars, though its numbers have declined steadily over the past century or more. Still seen regularly, especially during migration in spring, in late May and early June, and fall between late August and September, when they may be seen flying in loose groups just above the treetops on long, pointed wings with white bars near the tips. Breeds throughout the state on flat-topped gravel roofs, near blueberry barrens, or bare ground, rarely in southern Maine in recent decades but still fairly common Downeast. Call is a loud, nasal *peeent*, similar to that of the American Woodcock, and males in breeding season produce an unforgettable zooming sound by manipulating the airflow over their wings during a steep dive.

In flight note long, thin, pointed wings with white bars near the ends. Flight is erratic and bounding. Roosts during the day on a branch or phone wire, often in plain view but hidden by mottled brown camouflage.

Eastern Whip-poor-will

Antrostomus vociferus

L 10" | **WS** 19"

A rare and declining nightjar, the Eastern Whip-poor-will
prefers open, sandy woods with mixed conifers and deciduous
woods. A strictly nocturnal species, Eastern Whip-poor-wills
are rarely seen in migration—they're rarely seen at all, really,
as their mottled, cryptic patterning helps them disappear
into the leaf litter or along a low, horizontal branch for their
daytime roosts. Eastern Whip-poor-wills are best located by
their songs, an onomatopoeic, ceaseless *WHIP-piew-WEEW*.
Kennebunk Plains in York County and the Hothole Valley Parcel
of the Great Pond Mountain Wildlands in Hancock County are
perhaps the most reliable spots in Maine to hear them, though
they may have been recorded in suitable habitat in many locations outside of Aroostook County and dense northern forests.

Small and inconspicuous with
mottled grayish- or
reddish-brown plumage,
white or buffy corners to
outer tail. Best located by call.

Chimney Swift

Chaetura pelagica

L 5" | **WS** 11"

Chimney Swifts are familiar birds of cities and towns, seen
zipping through the sky on long, fluttering wings in pursuit
of flying insects. They are only seen in flight, as they choose to
roost communally inside inaccessible areas like hollow trees,
caves, and manmade chimneys. They arrive in Maine in late
April, announcing themselves with a constant, high-pitched
twittering, and depart in late August into the early part of
September. As with many aerial insectivores, Chimney Swift
numbers are in a marked decline, though huge numbers of
migrating swifts may still be seen gathering at dusk around a
certain chimney and all pouring in at once in an unforgettable
display.

"Cigars with wings," dusky
gray all over with lighter
throat, sickle-shaped wings.

Belted Kingfisher

Megaceryle alcyon

L 13" | **WS** 21"

A bold and dramatic species, Belted Kingfishers are widespread but fairly uncommon species across Maine, potentially found anywhere there is open water. They are year-round residents, breeding in summer by excavating burrows in dirt embankments and hunting by perching over water or hovering, and plunge diving onto prey. Migrates south towards coastal areas in September and October, and small numbers remain along the coast all winter. They can be easily overlooked when perched motionless at the water's edge, and their presence is often announced by a loud, hard rattle given in flight.

Dark blue-gray above, white below. Females show both a blue and rusty breast bands. Males have just a single breast band. White underwings, shaggy crest, and powerful bill.

Ruby-throated Hummingbird
Archilochus colubris

L 3" | **WS** 4"

The smallest bird in Maine and our only breeding hummingbird
species, the Ruby-throated Hummingbird is a welcome garden
visitor between early May and mid-September. Prefers red
tubular flowers, though also feeds readily from hummingbird
feeders, and also gleans insects from foliage, plucks spiders
from their webs, and drinks at holes chiseled in trees by Yellow-
bellied Sapsuckers. Adult males sport their namesake gorget,
which gleams red in direct light but can look dark from other
angles. Females are white below and green above, and young
males show scattered red feathers on their throat. Humming-
birds seen after mid-September may be any number of western
species, so look carefully. Call is a squeaky chittering sound
while hovering.

Glossy throat feathers
of breeding male may
look red, orange, or
black, depending on
light and angle. Note
black chin, dusky sides
to white belly.

The "Ruby-throat" is Maine's only expected hummingbird species, but any late fall or winter hummingbird should be closely scrutinized for stray western species.

Females and juveniles white below. Note white spots on ends of upperside of black tail feathers.

Red-bellied Woodpecker

Melanerpes carolinus

L 9" | **WS** 15"

Famously one of the most confusingly-named birds in America, those looking to identify the Red-bellied Woodpecker should look not for any color underneath but rather red on the top and back of the head, the strongly barred black-and-white back, and the cream-colored body and cheeks. There is a reddish smudge between the legs, but it's only easily seen when the bird is in hand, as it was for shotgun-bearing collectors of yore. The Red-bellied Woodpecker is a new arrival in Maine, a true rarity as recently as the late 1990s, now a fairly common year-round resident in southern and central Maine. Favors large deciduous trees in suburban forests, and regularly visits backyard bird feeders. Most frequently-heard calls are a loud, rolling *churrr* and a nasal, barking, squirrel-like *chig-chig-chig*.

Strongly barred black-and-white back, tan below and on cheeks, red crown and nape on male, tan crown and red nape on female.

Yellow-bellied Sapsucker

Sphyrapicus varius

L 8" | **WS** 15"

The Yellow-bellied Sapsucker is Maine's only member of this unusual family of woodpeckers which drill regularly-spaced holes in trees and then drink the sap and insects collected there. Though Yellow-bellied Sapsuckers are common only in summer their handiwork can be seen year around as patterned piercings in apple trees, maples, oaks, and other deciduous trees. The species arrives in April and breeds throughout the state, though more common outside of southern Maine, before departing in October. They are inconspicuous and easily over-looked in migration but make their presence known during breeding season with a loud, nasal mewing and an identifiable drumming, which starts quickly then slowly peters out.

Thin woodpecker with white vertical line along wing, black-and-white patterned head and back. Male has red cap and throat, female red cap and white throat.

American Three-toed Woodpecker

Picoides dorsalis

L 8.75" | **WS** 15"

A rare denizen of mature conifer forests in far northern Maine, the American Three-toed Woodpecker is one of the most sought-after breeding birds. Small and inconspicuous, American Three-toed Woodpeckers and their close northern cousins the Black-backed Woodpeckers, typically feed not by drilling holes but by peeling bark off trees in search of insects beneath. They are found most often on spruce and fir, especially in patches that have been damaged in some way: by fire, wind, or encroaching swampland. Most sightings in Maine come from remote logging roads north of Baxter State Park and mature forests in northern Aroostook County, though even there birders can go long stretches without seeing one. Calls include a flat *pwik*, a sharp series of chattered *piks*, and a strong drum which peters out at the end.

Males black and white with difficult-to-see yellow cap. White on back often less than shown in eastern birds.

Females lack yellow cap. Lack of white spots on wings helps distinguish from Hairy and Downy Woodpecker.

Black-backed Woodpecker
Picoides arcticus

L 9.5" | **WS** 16"

The Black-backed Woodpecker is a beautiful but inconspicuous woodpecker of conifer forests, with a larger range
in Maine than its close relative, the American Three-toed
Woodpecker. Like that species, the Black-backed Woodpecker
prefers to colonize stands of dead conifers, especially forests
that have been recently burned but also areas killed by insects
or encroaching beaver ponds. May spend long periods at one
tree, flaking bark in search of the wood-boring insect larvae,
and resulting flaky patches are a good indication that this
species may be present. Acadia National Park, Baxter State
Park, Katahdin Woods and Waters National Monument, and the
boreal forests around Rangeley, Topsfield, and northern Aroostook County are all areas to search. Calls include a sharp *pik*,
and drum is a solid series of knocks that trails off abruptly.

Only woodpecker with entirely black back.
Males with yellow cap, females without.
Single white stripe extends below eye.

Downy Woodpecker

Dryobates pubescens

L 6" | **WS** 11"

The pocket-sized Downy Woodpecker is Maine's smallest and most common woodpecker. Regularly found in a variety of habitats, including open deciduous woods, city parks, and backyard suet feeders. They prefer to hitch their way along trunks and branches in search of beetle larvae and other insects. Flight, as with all woodpeckers, is undulating: a series of rising flaps followed by a tucked-wing dip. This species regularly confused by the nearly identical Hairy Woodpecker, which is larger with a longer bill. The call is a sharp, descending whinny and a soft *pik*.

Small, black with white patch on back, white spots on wings, white belly and facial patterning. Males have red on back of head.

Females lack red patch. To separate from Hairy Woodpecker, note short bill barely extending beyond downy feather tuft, small dark spots on white outer tail feathers.

Hairy Woodpecker

Dryobates villosus

L 9" | **WS** 14"

A slightly-larger but otherwise nearly identical copy of the Downy Woodpecker, the Hairy Woodpecker is less common, and often prefers deeper woods and larger trees. Is common statewide, however, and may also appear at backyard suet feeders, so focus on longer bill and unmarked white outer tail feathers to distinguish from Downy. Calls include a sharp *peek*, higher-pitched than Downy, and a rattle on the same pitch, not descending in pitch.

Sturdy bill equals the length of head, comparatively longer than on Downy. Unmarked white outer tail feathers. Males with red head patch, absent in females. White wing spots and white patch on back.

Northern Flicker

Colaptes auratus

L 12" | **WS** 18"

Northern Flickers are a standout among the mostly black-and-white woodpeckers in Maine, a large, brownish bird with striking gold wing feathers and a white rump. A common migrant, Northern Flickers arrive in late March and breed throughout the state, preferring open woodlands like forest edges, golf courses, city parks and suburban areas. Prefers to feed on the ground, unlike other woodpeckers, hunting for ants and beetles in lawns and other mowed areas. In fall migration, September and early October, Northern Flickers may be seen in large numbers, especially along the coast and on offshore islands. Calls include a sharp kee-yer, and a loud *ick-ick-ick* given in spring, similar to Pileated Woodpecker but higher-pitched.

Brownish overall with black bars on back, red and gray on neck, and slightly decurved bill.

Strongly bounding flight shows bright yellow on wings and tail.

Male shows black line on face, female plain.

Pileated Woodpecker

Dryocopus pileatus

L 17" | **WS** 28"

Rare is the viewer who doesn't stop and marvel upon sighting a Pileated Woodpecker, an almost unbelievable species the size of a crow, with a bright red crest and a bill the size of a railroad spike. Found year-round throughout the state, though never common, it prefers mature forests and often forages low on stumps or dead trees, excavating large holes and leaving piles of wood chips behind. Often seen in flight, identified by large white patches on underwings and deep, rowing flight. Call is a loud, rapid *kuh-kuh-kuh-kuh-kuh* series, sounding perhaps gull-like or out of a jungle. Also gives loud, tentative *kuk* notes, often in flight.

The largest woodpecker in Maine. Excavates trees, often close to the ground, in search of insects.

Males show red stripe behind bill, black in females. Extensive white underwings in flight. Deep, rowing flight style.

Olive-sided Flycatcher

Contopus cooperi

L 7.5"   **WS** 13"

A large flycatcher with a distinctive "vested" appearance, the Olive-sided Flycatcher breeds in western and northern Maine, as well as Downeast, in Washington County. In decades past it bred throughout the state, but overall populations have declined more than 80% since the 1960s due to loss of habitat on the wintering grounds and insect declines. Arrives in Maine in mid-May and announces its presence: Olive-sided Flycatchers sit on prominent perches in tall trees, singing their famous "*Quick, Three Beers!*" song and making quick sallies for flying insects. They are one of the earliest migratory species to head southward, peaking in mid-August.

Drab-colored, with smudgy sides of breast giving a distinct "vested" look. White feather tufts on sides of rump occasionally exposed.

Eastern Wood-Pewee

Contopus virens

L 6" | **WS** 10"

Eastern Wood-Pewees are medium-sized flycatchers of deciduous woods, whose name derives from their clear, whistled song. The species arrives in late May and breeds throughout the state, though perhaps most common in southern and central Maine. It prefers to hunt flying insects in the canopy, making it sometimes harder to pick out than flycatchers that prefer open perches, like Olive-sided. As a result, Eastern Wood-Pewees are more easily heard than seen, its call is a forlorn *pee-a-WEE*, usually followed by a descending *peee-URR*.

Shows a pair of whitish wing bars with some white on flight feathers. Dingy gray overall, with dusky breast and crested look. Note the lack of an eye ring.

Yellow-bellied Flycatcher

Empidonax flaviventris

L 5.5" | **WS** 8"

Empidonax flycatchers, or "Empids," are a group of similar species differentiated by details of their calls, plumage, and habitat. The Yellow-bellied Flycatcher breeds in wet, boggy boreal forests. Arrives towards the end of May and disperses into heavily forested areas of eastern, western, and northern Maine. Locations to search in summer include the Rangeley and Sugarloaf areas in the eastern mountains, Moosehorn NWR in Washington County, and Baxter State Park and Katahdin Woods and Waters National Monument. Its namesake amber color is subtle, and may be lacking on worn birds, making Yellow-bellied Flycatcher easy to mix up with the similar Least Flycatcher. Vocalizations are important in all empidonax identifications, and the Yellow-bellied Flycatcher's song is a hoarse and sometimes trilled cheberk, more musical than the flat, dry song of the Least Flycatcher. Call is a shorebird-like *tuwee*.

Yellowish gray back, darker wings with white wing bars.

Yellowish color overall with yellowish throat, thin eyering.

Least Flycatcher

Empidonax minimus

L 5" | **WS** 8"

A small flycatcher of deciduous forests across the state, the Least Flycatcher hunts from lower in the forest than other woodland flycatchers. They're also pugnacious, known for aggressively escorting other birds from their territories, even species more than twice their size. But the Least Flycatcher's most distinguishing feature is its incessant singing in summer, an assertive, dry *cheBEC, cheBEC*. The species arrives in early May, and while still seen in good numbers, Least Flycatchers have experienced an 85% decline since the late 1960s in the United States. Look, and listen, for Least Flycatchers in mature deciduous woods with semi-open understory in summer, and at woodland edges in migration—when identification of all Empidonax flycatchers becomes very difficult due to a lack of vocalizations.

Small, olive-gray on back and whitish on breast, with small bill, complete eye ring, and white wing bars.

Alder Flycatcher

Empidonax alnorum

L 6" | **WS** 9"

Alder and Willow Flycatchers are two nearly identical species, best separated by differences in song. They were considered a single species, Traill's Flycatcher, until they were split in the early 1970's. Alder is a more common breeder of the two, especially outside of southern Maine, where it can be common in wet boreal forests and shrubby bogs. Reliable places to search for Alder Flycatchers between late April and mid-August include boreal forests around Rangeley, Baxter State Park and Katahdin Woods and Waters National Monument, Acadia National Park, the Bangor areas, and others. Song is a rough, rolled *rrreBEEA* or *free-BEEA*, with emphasis on the second syllable, and call is a flat pip. Not usually possible to separate from Willow Flycatcher in fall when not vocalizing.

Grayish-brown above, thin but distinct eye ring, wide-based bill, short wing tips, whitish wing bars, yellowish flanks.

Willow Flycatcher

Empidonax traillii

L 6" | **WS** 9"

Nearly identical to Alder Flycatcher, from which it cannot be reliably separated without vocalization. Willow Flycatcher is expanding its range in Maine, and is now relatively common along the southern coast up to Bangor. They stick close to willows, and are frequently seen hawking insects from brushy areas near water, such as the meadows of the Gilsland Farm Audubon Center in Falmouth, Laudholm Farm in Wells, and Penjajawog Marsh in Bangor, Song is a two-parted *FITZ-bew*, with emphasis on the first syllable, and call note is a liquid whit. Not usually possible to separate from Alder Flycatcher in fall when not vocalizing.

early identical to Alder Flycatcher,
ough eye ring is often less
stinct or absent. Grayish-brown
ove, whitish below. Prefers
rubby areas near water.

Eastern Phoebe

Sayornis phoebe

L 6″ | **WS** 10″

A nondescript but cheerful species, the Eastern Phoebe's return to Maine in late March is a welcome sign that spring is on the way. They thrive around human habitation, and readily nest under the eaves of homes, in barns, and under bridges before departing the state by early October. The Eastern Phoebe announces its presence by calling its own name (if only all birds were so generous): an emphatic and repeated *FEE-bee! FEE-belilip! FEE-bee!* Distinguished from other small flycatchers by its overall dark coloration, with faint or lacking wingbars, and habitat of wagging its tail when perched.

Small brown flycatcher, darker on face and head than on back. Juveniles have yellowish wash below.

Great Crested Flycatcher

Myiarchus crinitus

L 8" | **WS** 13"

The largest and most colorful flycatcher in Maine, the Great Crested Flycatcher is at the northern extent of its breeding range. Most common in the southern lowlands, from York County up through Bangor, the species nests in tree cavities or nest boxes, unlike any other flycatcher in the state. They generally arrive in mid-May, announcing themselves with a loud, rising *WHEEEP*, as well as a series of trilled, chirping calls, and have migrated south again by the middle of September. Listening for their song is typically how they are discovered, as they feed by sitting motionless high in the canopy before zipping out after a flying insect.

Medium-sized bird with brown head and back, gray cheeks and chest, yellow belly, and rust-colored wing feathers and undertail.

Eastern Kingbird

Tyrannus tyrannus

L 8" | **WS** 14"

A large and conspicuous flycatcher, the Eastern Kingbird is famous for its pugnacity on the breeding grounds, where it aggressively escorts much larger birds like hawks and crows from its territory. Prefers semi-open habitats with a mix of fields and trees, often near water, and is still relatively common in Maine despite a steep decline in the state due to a loss of such habitats coupled with a decline in flying insects. Arrives in late April to aggressively defend its territory but becomes quite social when headed south in September, and flocks of more than a dozen are not uncommon along the coast or on offshore islands. Song is a stuttered chirping, becoming more emphatic at its final notes: *dee-dee-dee-dee dee-DEE*, and call is a buzzy *kzeer*.

A handsome species, black above and white below, with characteristic white tips to black tail.

Northern Shrike

Lanius borealis

L 10" | **WS** 14.5"

Don't let its small stature fool you: the Northern Shrike is one of the most fearsome predators in the state. Northern Shrike and the others in its family are predatory songbirds with a taste for insects and small mammals, and a reluctance to let anything go to waste: they store excess food by impaling it on thorns, earning them the name "Butcher Birds." Northern Shrike are winter visitors to Maine, arriving in late October from tundra breeding grounds and spending the winter in open habitats like meadows, where it perches high atop bushes or trees to survey its hunting grounds. Numbers vary greatly from year to year, and never common, but good places to search include Laudholm Farm, East Point Audubon Sanctuary at Biddeford Pool, Great Salt Bay Farm Wildlife Preserve in Damariscotta, Penjajawog Marsh in Bangor, and other appropriate habitats.

Big headed bird often seen perched at the very top of a bush or tree in winter. Gray body, black wings, tail, and facemask, and strongly hooked bill.

Yellow-throated Vireo

Vireo flavifrons

L 6" | **WS** 9"

Vireos are a family of small songbirds known for their repetitive singing and preference for dense foliage. The Yellow-throated Vireo reaches the northern extent of its breeding range in southern Maine, and Brownfield Bog Wildlife Management Area in Oxford County is the most reliable location to find them during the breeding season. Uncommon anywhere but may be found in fall in small numbers on coastal islands like Monhegan. Most vireos are recognized by their oft-repeated songs, and the Yellow-throated Vireo gives a slow, burry, two-parted song, sounding like *THREE-eight, three-EIGHT, REE-year*, etc.

A chunky vireo with yellow on the front half, including conspicuous yellow "spectacles" around a black eye. White wing bars, and white belly and undertail.

Blue-headed Vireo

Vireo solitarius

L 6" | **WS** 9"

A smartly-dressed songbird, the white "spectacles" of the
Blue-headed Vireo contrast neatly with its blue-gray head.
An early migrant, these vireos begin returning to Maine in
early April and occupy a wide variety of forests throughout
the state, where it moves deliberately through the canopy
gleaning insects from leaves. Though never abundant, may be
easily found in many locations in summer, especially outside of
southern Maine, at spots including Hidden Valley Nature Center
in Jefferson, Baxter State Park and Katahdin Woods and Waters
National Monument, and the Bangor City Forest. Lingers until
mid-October, one of the later-leaving songbirds. Song is a series
of sweet phrases, well-spaced, sounding like "*hear me, see me,
here I am.*" Oft-heard alarm call is a grating chatter.

Large-headed, with bright
white spectacles against a
slate blue head, greenish
flanks with white belly, white
wing bars and green back.

Warbling Vireo

Vireo gilvus

L 5" | **WS** 9"

A subtle and easily overlooked species, the Warbling Vireo is an uncommon breeder in Maine away from coniferous forests in the west, northwest, and Downeast. The species has something of a reputation for featurelessness, but birders should focus on its plain face with "ghost spectacles" arching above and below its black eye. That's if you can spot it: the Warbling Vireo spends its time high in deciduous trees, often near water, and is typically located by its namesake song. Found mostly in southern Maine, reliable locations include Capisic Pond Park in Portland, Gilsland Farm Audubon Center, Sanford Lagoons, Unity Pond, and Essex Woods in Bangor, and is increasing in the hills of Aroostook County, including Lake Josephine. Song is a sweet, rapid warble, similar to House Finch but faster and usually ending on a high note, also utters a descending, raspy scold.

Plain brownish gray overall, slight yellow wash below, with faint white arches above and below eye.

Philadelphia Vireo

Vireo philadelphicus

L 5″ | **WS** 9″

A lovely but scarce breeder in northern Maine, the Philadelphia Vireo may go under-detected due to difficulties distinguishing its song from the more common Red-eyed Vireo. Philadelphia Vireos migrate north in mid-May and seek young deciduous forests in western and northern Maine, the southern edge of one of the most northern breeding vireos. Coastal including Evergreen Cemetery in Portland, Monhegan Island, and Biddeford Pool are good spots to search during migration, while early and mid-age deciduous woods with aspens, birches, and alders is best during the breeding season, such as is found around Rangeley and in Baxter State Park. Song is a series of whistled phrases very similar to the Red-eyed Vireo but generally higher-pitched and with longer pauses.

Small and stocky, wash yellow underneath is often best field mark, though not always evident.

Red-eyed Vireo

Vireo olivaceus

L 5" | **WS** 10"

The Red-eyed Vireo is a widespread and chatty species found in almost any forest habitat in the state during the summer. Arriving in May, the Red-eyed Vireo's cheerful and nonstop song of whistled phrases can be heard, unlike most other songbirds, through the heat of the day. Summer birders may need to settle for the song, as Red-eyed Vireos can be tough to spot as they glean insects high in tree canopies, but the species is often very abundant and obliging in fall migration, especially along the coast. Song is a continuous ramble of typically three-note phrases, often remembered as sounding like *here-I-am, look-at-me, at-the-top, look-up,* etc.

Olive-green above, white below, with long bill. Gray crown with dark border and dark line through red eye distinctive.

Horned Lark

Eremophila alpestris

L 7" | **WS** 13"

Horned Larks are a fairly common but easily overlooked species of barren, open ground. Is an uncommon breeder in the state, known from just a few spots including airports and beaches in southern and central Maine and agricultural fields in Aroostook County. More common in winter, when flocks may be found on beaches and salt marshes along the southern coast, such as Scarborough Marsh, hotspots between Wells and Kennebunkport, and the Biddeford Pool area. Flocks march inconspicuously along the ground and are often difficult to pick out until the birds take flight, making a series of one or two syllable, tinkling or bell-like notes.

Brownish overall with distinctive black and yellow face pattern, and small feathered "horns." Yellow on the face variable.

Canada Jay

Perisoreus canadensis

L 11.5" | **WS** 18"

A subtlety-plumaged but charismatic species of boreal forests,
the Canada Jay goes by many names, including Gray Jay,
Whiskey Jack, Camp Robber, and Gorby. Small family groups
of this species may be spotted gliding through dense coniferous
woods in search of food. They inhabit Maine's western mountains, northern forests, and the boreal woods of far Downeast
Maine, and likely spots include the Rangeley area, Baxter State
Park and Katahdin Woods and Waters National Monument, the
Burn Road in Topsfield, and the the Moosehorn NWR, among
others. Though typically quieter than most jays and crows, Canada
Jays have a range of calls including harsh squawks, clear whistles,
chatters, and they're also known to mimic other species.

Large and fluffy, with
grayish body, white
face, and dark cap.
Alternates rapid wing
beats with slow, glided
flight. Juveniles all lead
gray, often with whitish
stripe extending from
bill.

Blue Jay

Cyanocitta cristata

L 11" │ **WS** 15"

The Blue Jay is one of Maine's most familiar and ubiquitous species, yet somehow also under appreciated for its tropical beauty, cunning, and vocal repertoire. A year-round resident, though numbers vary seasonally depending on food availability, Blue Jays are most common in southern Maine but found in woods across the state, particularly near oak trees. Acorns are a favorite food, but Blue Jays also eat insects, grains, backyard birdseed, small dead invertebrates, and, occasionally, eggs and nestlings from the nests of other birds. Related to crows, they share an advanced intelligence, as illustrated through tight family bonds, complex vocalizations, and, in captive birds at least, tool use. Calls include the familiar *jeer jeer*, a squeaky *TEEleelee*; and even spot-on imitations of Red-shouldered and Red-tailed Hawks.

Large and blue, with variable black bridle and neck band. White on tail and inner wings in flight. Crest held low when relaxed, erect when agitated.

Common Raven

Corvus corax

L 24" | **WS** 46"

Common Ravens are large, powerful birds that have made a remarkable recovery since their extirpation from the state in the 1800s. Now they may be found nesting anywhere in the state in low numbers, but perhaps are most evident in more remote areas where there are few crows and where the raven's guttural calls may be heard from a great distance. May be seen almost anywhere, though, and are best distinguished from the similar American Crow by larger size and long, wedge-shaped tail. Many different vocalizations are known—more than 30 categories of vocalization, in fact—but most commonly heard is a deep, growling croak, but also shrill whistles, bell-like *dongs* and clicks, and many more.

Very large, all black, with long, heavy bill about half covered in feathers.

Long, wedge-shaped tail
unlike American Crow.
Long, narrow wings.

Gives a remarkable variety of vocalizations.
The most common, a gurgling croak, can be
heard from more than a mile away.

American Crow

Corvus brachyrhynchos

L 18" | **WS** 37"

The American Crow is one of the most common and familiar birds in Maine, a boisterous companion in nearly any habitat all year-round. Though most common near areas of human disturbance, such as agricultural fields, suburban woodlands and yards, cities and towns, American Crows may be found nearly anywhere. Their most remarkable scenes occur in winter, when breeding-season territoriality is over and crows move at dusk to roost communally, sometimes in sky-filling (and ominous, to non-birders) flocks of up to several thousands birds. Less numerous inland during the winter, when birds move closer to the coast. Maine hosts spring and fall no-limit hunting seasons for crows, with different dates depending on location, though they are not popular as a game bird. American Crows have a number of vocalizations, most famously their deep *caw-caw-caw*, but also including croaks, bell-like sounds, knocks, and rattles.

Large and all black, often seen in small groups. Broad wings, short, rounded tail. Flies with smooth, "rowing" wing beats.

Fish Crow

Corvus ossifragus

L 15" | **WS** 33"

The Fish Crow is a nearly-identical relative of the American Crow that is slowly expanding its breeding range north into the state. Present now only along the coast of southern Maine beginning in early spring, Fish Crows are often associated with parking lots and similar developed areas, especially near water. Reliable locations include Pine Point in Scarborough, Laudholm Farm in Wells, Ogunquit, Brunswick, and up the coast to Rockland. Fish Crows average slightly smaller than American Crows, with shorter legs, though visual identification is very challenging. Voice is the most reliable method to distinguish the two species, as the Fish Crow eschews the caw and utters a short, nasal *anh, anh-ah* or *cah, cah-ah*.

Very similar to American Crow, though a bit smaller, glossier, with shorter legs and bill. Listen for simple nasal call.

Purple Martin
Progne subis

L 8" | **WS** 16"

The large Purple Martin dazzles with its aerial acrobatics as it hunts flying insects through the air. However, this once statewide species has declined more than 90% in Maine since the late 1960s due, it's thought, to a combination of prey declines, a loss of traditional nesting areas, and competition from invasive cavity-nesters like House Sparrow and European Starling. Today, Purple Martins in the eastern U.S. next almost exclusively in man-made objects, like hollow gourds or elaborately-decorated houses, a tradition dating back to the Native Americans. Fewer than 20 Purple Martin colonies remain in Maine, scattered from York County to western Penobscot County. They migrate in late April from breeding grounds below the Equator, and return in July and August. Vocal around colonies, their song is a collection of throaty gurgles and laser-like noises.

Males are glossy purple all over, with long wings. Tail shallowly forked when not spread.

Females and immature birds show variable speckled gray and dingy brown below.

Tree Swallow

Tachycineta bicolor

L 6″ | **WS** 13″

A shining emerald found during a Maine summer over a variety of open habitats in Maine, including meadows, ponds, rivers, and marshes. Tree Swallows have experienced the overall population declines of many insectivorous birds, but remain common throughout Maine. They arrive in early March and take up residence in tree cavities and man made nest boxes, and migrate south between July and October. Peaking migration numbers in September are often represented by massive flocks, up to 5,000 strong, typically over water at locations including Biddeford Pool, Scarborough Marsh, and Christina Reservoir in Aroostook County. Small numbers may be seen late into the fall or winter along the southern coast, feeding on berries. Song is a high-pitched mix of chirps, whines, and gurgles, and calls include a rapid set of chirps.

Male is small, with a brilliant blue-green back and neat white below, with a sharp division between colors on the head. Short, broad wings and shallowly notched tail.

Females brownish above with some hints of blue. Juvenile birds may have smudgy breasts, potentially confusing with Bank Swallow.

Northern Rough-winged Swallow

Stelgidopteryx serripennis

L 6" | **WS** 11"

Confined to southern Maine, the Northern Rough-winged Swallow is a small, brown swallow with a dusky brown throat, lacking the color and contrast of the rest of our swallows. It arrives around late April and take up residence in burrows, crevices, and drainpipes, always near water. Good places to look for this smooth-flying swallow include Gilsland Farm Audubon Center, spots along Merrymeeting Bay, Weskeag Marsh, and the Messalonskee Boat Ramp. Call is a high, flatulent *brrt brrt*.

Plain brown above, with white undertail just visible.

Plain gray-brown below, fading to a white bellow and undertail. Short-tailed and broad-winged.

Bank Swallow

Riparia riparia

L 5" | **WS** 11"

Numbers of this small swallow have experienced a dizzying decline in recent decades, and their population currently sits at around 1% of its numbers from the late 1960s. Still fairly common in southern Maine, where they may be found nesting in colonies dug into the sides of riverbanks or vertical bluffs near water. Still reliably seen at Laudholm Farm, along Eastern Road at Scarborough Marsh, the Messalonskee Lake area, and others. Distinguished from Northern Rough-winged Swallow and immature Tree Swallows by sharply contrasting brown breast band and white throat. The typical flight call is a harsh, rapid *tschr tschr*.

Solid brown above with brown breast band contrasting against white throat. Long, slender tail in flight.

Cliff Swallow

Petrochelidon pyrrhonota

L 5″ | **WS** 12″

Cliff Swallows are stocky, blue and orange swallows famous for building mud nests under bridges and eaves. Like most aerial insectivores they have experienced a steady decline since the middle of the 20th century, but Cliff Swallows may still be found statewide. Look for them anywhere swallows congregate, or tending to their mud nests at the Nesowadnehunk Campground at Baxter State Park, at Green Point WMA in Lincoln County, near Scarborough Marsh, or even in downtown Bangor. Calls include a sharp, descending *veerr*.

Stocky blue swallow with a dark red throat, buff patch above bill, and pale reddish rump. May be seen collecting mud to build nest.

Barn Swallow

Hirundo rustica

L 7" | **WS** 12"

The elegant Barn Swallow is one of the most recognizable birds in the world. Flocks of these swallows zipping over fields or water just a few inches off the surface, their long, forked tails flaring as they turn, are a familiar sight in appropriate habitats across the state. Arriving in April and gone by October, Barn Swallows nest almost exclusively on human structures, including barns, eaves, and under bridges. It's reliance on human structures means that Barn Swallows are uncommon away from them, such as in the heavily forested parts of the state. Song is a series of squeaky notes interrupted by a dry rattle, calls include a high-pitched and oft-repeated *cheep*.

Flight on long pointed wings is often rapid, low, and direct. Dark blue above, orange below, darker on throat. Long forked tail.

Black-capped Chickadee
Poecile atricapillus

L 5" | **WS** 8"

In their 1927 proposal to establish a State Bird for Maine, the State Federation of Women's Clubs wrote that chickadees expressed the "qualities of optimism, cheeriness, friendliness, resourcefulness, and industry," which "stand forth as qualities of the citizens of Maine." Without worrying about the scientific accuracy of that observation (or questioning whether Mainers are generally cheery and optimistic), there's no doubt that the familiar Black-capped Chickadee is a beloved bird, whether seen at a backyard feeder or in the deep woods. The species is a cavity nester, and will readily take to man made nest boxes, beginning usually in May. This social species has a complex language of vocalizations. The song, heard in early spring, is a clear, two parted *FEE-BEE*, with the second note lower; the most common call is the onomatopoeic *chick-a-dee-dee*, an alarm call with the number of "dees" on the end corresponding to the intensity of the threat.

Easily recognizable black and white facial pattern, pinkish wash on flanks, white edges to wing and tail feathers.

In 1927, the State Federation of Women's Clubs said the chickadee "stays here the year around, is friendly and easily attracted to human beings, and according to entomologists is one of the greatest destroyers of insects and plant destroyers."

Chickadees frequently cache seeds for later consumption.

Boreal Chickadee

Poecile hudsonicus

L 5" | **WS** 8"

Maine's other chickadee, Boreal Chickadee are an uncommon
resident of spruce-fir forests outside of southern and central
Maine. It's remote habitats and reluctance to visit bird feeders
make it a challenging bird to find, but Saddleback Mountain
and the Rangeley area, Baxter State Park and Katahdin Woods
and Waters National Monument, Quoddy Head SP, and the
Muscovic Road in Aroostook County are reliable locations to
search. Boreal Chickadees are year-round residents and, like
Black-capped Chickadees, cache seeds during the summer and
fall to be eaten in winter. The song is higher pitched than that
of the Black-capped Chickadee, with which Boreal Chickadees
sometimes mingle, a mechanical *tsee-a-dee-dee*, and a nasal
note: *jayyy jayyyy*.

Darker than Black-
capped Chickadee,
with a brown cap, gray
nape, and no white
edges on wings.

Tufted Titmouse

Baeolophus bicolor

L 6" | **WS** 9"

This southern species is quickly expanding its range in Maine, first seen along the southern coast in the 1980s and now expanding north to Franklin County, and east to Bangor, Mount Desert Island, and even Washington County. A common resident where it is found, Tufted Titmice are readily seen at backyard bird feeders in deciduous woodlands and wooded suburbs. Naturally found in excavated woodpecker holes, titmice take readily to bird boxes and often line them with hair plucked from living mammals. Their song seems unusually loud for their small stature, a clear, whistled *PE-TER PE-TER, PE-TER*, heard most often in late winter or early spring. Also makes a buzzy scold call when mobbing predators, or prying birders.

Gray above, white below, with black eye standing out on white face, black forehead and orange flanks.

White-breasted Nuthatch

Sitta carolinensis

L 5.5" | **WS** 10"

The White-breasted Nuthatch is a charismatic species, creeping along tree trunks and large branches and probing crevices for insects. They are primarily birds of deciduous woodlands, and so are less common in some of the state's northern and eastern coniferous stands, but are otherwise found throughout the state as a permanent resident. Typically forages in a downward direction, clinging to the bark and bouncing headfirst down a tree, but also readily visits bird feeders and suet cages. Song is a monotone, repeated *weh-weh-weh-weh-weh-weh-weh*, and call is high, nasal inh inh notes while foraging.

Stocky and neckless, with gray cap, slate blue back, and white underparts. Rusty undertail, and white in wings and tail visible during the nuthatch's undulating flight.

Red-breasted Nuthatch

Sitta canadensis

L 4.5" | **WS** 8"

The charming Red-breasted Nuthatch is a permanent, year round resident in Maine, favoring coniferous woods. Smaller than its white-breasted cousin and one of the smallest songbirds in the state, the Red-breasted Nuthatch zig-zag rapidly down and up tree branches looking for insects, and also regularly visit feeders. Numbers vary in winter: in some years when the cone crop is poor in northerly latitudes the species "irrupts" south into southern Maine and coastal island (and sometimes much further), beginning early fall. The call is a slow, nasal *ANNK ANNK ANNK*, as if the species is practicing just a single note on a toy trumpet.

Very small. Blue back and orange/red below, with sharply contrasting black and white facial pattern.

Brown Creeper

Certhia americana

L 5" | **WS** 7"

A very small songbird with cryptic plumage helping it to blend in with tree bark, the Brown Creeper starts low on the trunk and picks its way upward before flying low to the next tree. They prefer large deciduous trees for foraging, and build their nests beneath a large piece of flaking bark on a dead or dying tree. Widespread in Maine, but more common in the central and south than in the far north and Downeast. Vocalizations are extremely high-pitched, sometimes escaping those without perfect hearing. The song is a mix of sweet notes sounding like trees trees beautiful trees, and call note is a high whistled *seeeet*.

Tiny, thin, and well-camouflaged, with long tail braced against tree trunk. Buffy band on wing visible in flight.

Carolina Wren

Thryothorus ludovicianus

L 5 "   **WS** 8 "

Maine is the northern extent of the breeding range for the
Carolina Wren, which, as its name implies, has expanded out of
the southeast. It is fairly common in southern and Mid-Coast
Maine up through Mount Desert Island, its further expansion limited by the impacts of snow and severe winters on its
insect prey. They are at home in dense brush, typically low to
the ground, and like most wrens are known for their vigorous
and loud defense of their territory. Their song is a ringing
TEA-kettle, TEA-kettle, TEA-kettle; and notes include a bubby,
descending *cheeeeer*, raspy scolds, and drawn-out rattles.

Rusty-brown above and buffy below,
and white throat. Large white eye
stripe is the most prominent feature.

House Wren

Troglodytes aedon

L 5" | **WS** 7"

House Wrens reach the northeastern limit of their nationwide range in central Maine, and their bubbly songs and jittery demeanor are familiar in suburban backyards and lightly wooded areas south of Bangor. House Wrens arrive in May and are aggressive nesters known to evict larger species from nest boxes, such as Eastern Bluebirds or Tree Swallows. They aggressively defend their territories, chasing birds, squirrels, and other interlopers away before returning to hunt for insects in brush piles, shrubs, and other low areas. Both males and females sing a fast, jittery song of high-pitched notes, chatters, chirps, and scolds; call note is a rapid buzz.

Small, grayish-brown all over, with brown-barred wings and tail. Often found low in brush piles and tangles, often near humans.

Winter Wren

Troglodytes hiemalis

L 4" | **WS** 6"

A tiny, mouselike bird, the Winter Wren is fairly common in coniferous forests throughout the state, especially outside of southern Maine. They prefer mature forests, where they hop along fallen logs and under exposed roots in search of insects. Reliable summer locations include Acadia National Park, Baxter State Park, Katahdin Woods and Waters National Monument, Bangor City Forest, and other deep woods areas. Their small size and secluded habitats mean that they are generally heard before (or rather than) seen, their song an almost impossibly fast series of high-pitched trills and warbles, like a fiddle solo from an over-caffeinated mouse. Call is a barking *klip*.

Tiny, round, and all over dark brown with dark barring. Usually seen with tail held cocked.

Marsh Wren

Cistothorus palustris

L 5" | **WS** 7"

The Marsh Wren is a charismatic species of marshes filled with cattails, bulrush, sedges, and phragmites. They arrive in mid-May to wetlands from about Bangor south, where they remain into October. They can be difficult to see as they feed among the vegetation, clinging acrobatically to separate reeds with each foot, but males make short flights above the marsh and flutter back down in an attempt to impress females. Scarborough Marsh is a stronghold in Cumberland County, but they are also reliable in Great Salt Bay Farm Wildlife Preserve in Damariscotta, Messalonskee Lake in Belgrade, and Essex Woods and Penjajawoc Marsh in Bangor. Their song is a stuttery, harsh, gurgling trill, and note is a dry *check, check*.

Prominent eye stripe over eye on dark brown head. White streaks on black back. Tail typically held cocked, taller than head.

Blue-gray Gnatcatcher
Polioptila caerulea

L 4" | **WS** 6"

A tiny, long-tailed songbird, the Blue-gray Gnatcatcher is limited to moist, deciduous forests in southern Maine. Only a breeder in the state since the late 1970s, the species may slowly be continuing its expansion, especially along the coast. Blue-gray Gnatcatchers are a miniature bird that makes an outsized impression, constantly giving its nasal, descending speee notes and waving its long black-and-white tail as it flits through trees after insects. Uncommon along the coast in migration as far as Mount Desert Island, the Blue-gray Gnatcatcher's few reliable summer locations include Brownfield Bog WMA, Kennebunk Plains, and River Point Conservation Area in Falmouth. Song is a seemingly random series of thin wheezes, chatters, and *zee* notes.

Bluish-gray above, white below, white eye ring, black-and-white tail and black on wings. Male has black forehead, giving an "angry eyebrow" look. Females and young birds lack black forehead.

Golden-crowned Kinglet

Regulus satrapa

L 4" | **WS** 6"

A tiny year-round resident in Maine, Golden-crowned Kinglets move into coniferous forests in the western mountains, north, and Downeast for the breeding season. Their cascading songs belie their presence, hidden in the upper branches, in places like Acadia National Park, the Rangeley area, Moosehorn NWR, and Baxter State Park and Katahdin Woods and Waters National Monument. They disperse in winter and become more common in southern Maine and along the coast, though still may be found anywhere in the state, often mixing with flocks of chickadees, nuthatches, and other hearty winter denizens. The high-pitched song is a rollercoaster ride: a few slow rising notes reach a peak and descend rapidly in a descending chatter. Call note is a piercing metallic squeak: *tsee-tsee*.

Smaller than chickadees, with greenish above and grayish below, with black and white facial pattern and yellow (female) or orange (male) crest not always conspicuous.

Ruby-crowned Kinglet

Corthylio calendula

L 4" | **WS** 7"

The Ruby-crowned Kinglet is a common breeding species in mature spruce-fir forests throughout the state except for southern Maine. The lack of head stripes helps distinguish Ruby-crowned Kinglets from their Golden-crowned cousins, but this fairly drab species may often be mistaken for some of the greenish warblers or Empidonax flycatchers. The most helpful field mark isn't the namesake red head feathers, which are typically concealed, but rather the thick white and black wing bars and yellow-edged wing feathers. Arriving between mid-April and mid-May, and departing by mid-October, Ruby-crowned Kinglets stand out from a flock with their constant activity and wing-flickering behavior. Song begins with a series of slow, rising notes building to a prolonged tumble: *see, see, see dee-doo-dle, dee-doo-dle, dee-doo-dle*; note a quick, low *jidit*.

Olive green all over, with pale eyering most visible in front and behind eye. Thick white and black wing bars, yellow edges to wing feathers. Red crown on male only, usually hidden unless agitated.

Eastern Bluebird

Sialia sialis

L 7" | **WS** 12"

Eastern Bluebirds have become increasingly common in Maine over the past few decades, even in winter, much to the delight of suburban or semi-rural Mainers lucky enough to have these cheerful thrushes as neighbors. A bird of open country, farmland, orchards, and golf courses, especially those where specialty nest boxes have been erected, Eastern Bluebirds are more common in central and southern Maine and Aroostook County than in heavily forested or mountainous regions of the state. Winter numbers growing, though currently confined mainly to the coast from Bangor and Blue Hill south, where they switch from an insectivorous diet to fruit or backyard birdseed. Song is a pleasant collection of hoarse phrases, *chiti WEEW weediwew-widi* or similar. Call, often given in flight, is a simple, looping whistle.

Male bright blue above, rusty orange on breast, and white on belly.

Juveniles dark overall, heavily spotted on back and breast, with some blue feathering on wings and tail.

Female muted: pale blue above, lighter orange below.

Veery
Catharus fuscescens

L 7" | **WS** 11"

Each of the six species of *Catharus* and *Hylocichla* thrushes possible in Maine (including the rare Gray-cheeked Thrush, not covered here) show some combination of brown body and spotted breast. The species are distinguished by the shades of brown on the back, the saturation of the breast spots, details of the face and other marks, and by comparison of these species' gorgeous, flute-like songs. The Veery is the most reddish of these birds, and has the faintest breast spots. It arrives in mid-May and seeks out willow thickets and other dense shrubby areas in wet forests throughout the state. A generally shy and retiring bird, the Veery is readily identified by its song, an ethereal whistle which "veers" downward, memorably likened to the sound of a video game character dying. Note is a smooth *VE-er*.

Plain reddish brown above, large dark eye on plain face, very lightly spotted below.

Bicknell's Thrush

Catharus bicknelli

L 7" | **WS** 11.5"

One of the rarest and most sought-after species in Maine, the Bicknell's Thrush breeds only in stunted spruce or fir forests at the treeline of the state's tallest mountains. Bicknell's Thrush are rare in migration in late May and early June, and may be impossible to distinguish from another migrant thrush, the Gray-cheeked Thrush, without hearing vocalizations. For most, the only way to find a sure-fire Bicknell's Thrush in Maine is to hike to the top of Saddleback, Sugarloaf, Katahdin, Old Speck, and just a handful of other peaks, best in early morning, and listen for the bird's four-phrased, wiry, electric, fluted song. Bicknell's Thrush is listed as a Species of Special Concern in Maine, with major threats including loss of habitat on its Caribbean wintering grounds and the impacts of climate change on its already-limited breeding habitats. Call note is a clear, descending *peer* or *queeep*.

Plain brown, with brown spots on tan or whitish chest, fading towards belly and flanks.

Swainson's Thrush

Catharus ustulatus

L 7" | **WS** 12"

The Swainson's Thrush is a common migrant throughout the
state and an abundant and vocal breeding bird in the forests of
western, northern, and far eastern Maine. Distinguished from
other Catharus thrushes in migration by the buff coloration on
the face, which forms bold "spectacles." Swainson's Thrushes
migrate through southern Maine in mid-May and may be
glimpsed hopping through the leaf litter as with other thrushes,
or can also be detected by their Spring Peeper-like peep uttered
while flying overhead at night. They are inconspicuous on territory, but their gorgeous song of upward-spiraling, breezy, fluted
phrases may be heard in coniferous forests from the Rangeley
area through Baxter SP and Katahdin Woods and Waters NM up
through the Canadian border, as well as Mount Desert Island and
much of Hancock and Washington Counties though, in general,
breeding range is shifting northward and higher in elevation.

Brown above, whitish
below, with heavily-
spotted chest and buffy
face, neck, and eye-ring
give a "spectacled" look.

Hermit Thrush

Catharus guttatus

L 7" | **WS** 11"

The Hermit Thrush is the most common of the spotted thrushes in Maine, and the most likely species to be seen in winter. The species arrives in April and breeds throughout the state, foraging in the leaf litter or in the understory of many types of forests, before engaging in a drawn-out migration which sees most of the birds gone by early November, but some lingering through the winter, especially near the coast. Famously evocative song is eerier and more melancholy than its Catharus cousins, and usually begins with a clear, thin whistle followed by a series of fluted notes, thought to sound like *oh holy holy, oh sweetie sweetie*. Oft-heard call note is a quick *tchip*, or a whiny, rising *eeee*.

Reddish coloration on tail is best distinguishing feature. Otherwise brown all over with bold breast spots. Often raises and lowers tail upon landing.

Wood Thrush

Hylocichla mustelina

L 8" | **WS** 13"

The largest of Maine's spot-breasted thrushes is, unlike the others, most common in southern Maine. The richly-colored Wood Thrush inhabits the understory of mature deciduous forests from about Bangor and Mount Desert Island south, though the species has endured a decline in recent decades due in large part to habitat fragmentation. Reliable locations include Sieur de Monts Spring in Acadia National Park, Evergreen Cemetery in Portland, Fort Foster Park in Kittery, and Camden Hills SP. The species is most often heard before it is seen, its multi-parted, flute-like song begins with a rapid (and difficult to hear) *po-po-po* before launching into loud clear notes often including an *ee-oh-lay* and finishing with a liquid rattle; common call note are rapid, explosive *pit pit pit*.

Richly reddish brown with a large white belly marked with bold brown spots.

American Robin

Turdus migratorius

L 10" | **WS** 14"

The ubiquitous and well-loved American Robin may be found in almost any habitat in Maine, from urban parks and suburban lawns to offshore islands or the top of Mount Katahdin. Though in some places considered a sign of spring, robins are increasingly common in the winter, especially along the coast, where their diet shifts from worms to berries and fruit and where large flocks roost together. The species disperses throughout the state in spring, joined by southern migrants, to breed across the state, though less commonly in forests. They are a very vocal species, and in spring they are one of the earliest birds singing in the morning (before sunrise) and latest at night. Song is a string of loud, clear whistled phrases: *cheerily, cheer-up, cheerio, cheer-up*. Calls include a sharp *yeep* alarm call, and a whinnying laugh.

Adult bird is large and long-legged with rusty orange chest, blackish head, and yellow bill. Shows white tail corners in flight. Female paler orange on breast than male.

Juvenile birds seen May to September, with spotted orange breast, varying white on head.

Gray Catbird
Dumetella carolinensis

L 9" | **WS** 11"

A shy but amiable summer resident, the Gray Catbird is common in dense shrubs, brushy forests, and backyard underbrush most anywhere in Maine except deep forests. The species arrives in May to scour thickets for insects and berries, with males only pausing to sing from an exposed perch or aggressively see off intruders. Fall migration begins in mid-August and continues through October, with a small but growing number of individuals present throughout the winter, nearly always along the coast. Song is a squeaky jumble of rambling phrases; calls include their namesake, catlike *meeurr*, a several-note rapid chatter, and a dry *whurf*.

Gray overall with blackish cap and maroon undertail feathers. Thin and long-tailed. Active and vocal despite spending most of its time hidden in dense vegetation searching for fruit and insects.

Brown Thrasher

Toxostoma rufum

L 11″ | **WS** 12″

Brown Thrashers are a boldly-patterned but inconspicuous species that stay out of sight in dense brush near dry or sandy shrubland, powerline cuts, or blueberry barrens in eastern Maine. The species arrives in April and may be found through southern and central Maine and coastal Washington County, and less commonly through the less-forested parts of Aroostook County. Reliable locations in spring and summer include Kennebunk Plains, the Viles Arboretum in Augusta, Unity Pond, Gilsland Farm Audubon Center in Falmouth, Laudholm Farm, and the Rachel Carson NWR, where males may sit on exposed perches to sing. They are accomplished mimics, and their songs are known to include more than one thousand song types, delivered as couplets. Brown Thrashers also call with a low *chuck*.

Rusty brown above, two wing bars, breast strongly marked with dark streaks and spots. Long downcurved bill and bright yellow eye.

Northern Mockingbird

Mimus polyglottos

L 9" | **WS** 13"

The Northern Mockingbird is growing increasingly common in Maine. Once rare and considered a southern speciality, it is now a regular breeding species up through Bangor and Mount Desert Island, and local elsewhere in Maine save for northwestern Maine. Preferring open areas like suburbs or cemeteries, Northern Mockingbirds are best known for their mimicry, which includes spot-on impressions of Blue Jays, Killdeer, hawks, finches, sparrows, and many other species. If there's a Northern Mockingbird around you'll probably know it: they are loud and relentless singers, they sit on prominent perches, they actively and aggressively defend nesting and feeding territories, and the bright white patches on their wings are prominent in flight. Incessant song may be heard day or night, and consists of often mimicked phrases repeated several times before switching. Note is a dry *chak*.

Slate gray above, lighter below, wings and tail darker with obvious white wing bars. Often hunts on the ground, sometimes spreading wings to scare insect prey, revealing bold white patches on outer wing feathers, seen above and below.

American Pipit

Anthus rubescens

L 6″ | **WS** 11″

This open-ground bird nests in only one location in Maine: the treeless summit of Mount Katahdin. Inconspicuous flocks migrate through in April and May, stopping over at beaches, marshes, airports, and beaches on their way to the Arctic tundra. Just a few pairs each year make their summer home atop the state's tallest mountain, where males may be seen flying above the tablelands singing their song of high, clear phrases. Most common in Maine during fall migration, which extends from September into November, when small flocks of pipits may be found walking briskly across open ground in search of insects and seeds, especially along the coast. Brunswick Landing, Eastern Road at Scarborough Marsh, Biddeford Pool, Kettle Cove in Cape Elizabeth, and Laudholm Farm are all fairly regular fall stopover sites. Call is a sharp *pip-it* or *pip-pip*, usually given in flight.

Tall, brownish bird with varied amounts of breast streaking. Walks with a proud, head-bobbing strut.

European Starling

Sturnus vulgaris

L 8" | **WS** 14"

100 European Starlings were set loose in New York's Central Park in 1890 and they've grown to become one of the most abundant birds in the nation, with a population estimated to be 200 million. They were first reported in Maine in 1913 and were common in the state by 1930. Today they are common in all but the most remote parts of the state, including forest clearings far from human development, but are especially common near cities, towns, and agricultural areas. European Starlings are cavity nesters, and usually outcompete Tree Swallows, Eastern Bluebirds, Wood Ducks, Great Crested Flycatchers, and other species for man made boxes or natural tree cavities. Massive coordinated murmurations, performed after the nesting season, are a sight to behold. Song is an excited series of chips, rattles, whistles, squeaks, and pops; calls include a variety of chatters and grating notes.

Breeding starling is glossy purple-black with oily iridescent plumage and yellow bill. Distinct triangular shape in flight.

Juveniles are smudgy gray with streaks on belly and black bill, often seen mixed into adult flocks in summer.

House Sparrow

Passer domesticus

L 6" | **WS** 9"

Native to Eurasia and North Africa, the House Sparrow was introduced into the northeast U.S. in the late 1800s and has expanded to become one of the most numerous birds on the continent. They are common and widespread in Maine, but avoid forests and uninhabited areas and instead stay close to towns, cities, and agricultural areas. A hearty species, House Sparrows manage to hang on through tough winters by roosting communally in dense vegetation. They nest in early spring in cavities or nest boxes, and are considered a major threat to native cavity nesting species like Eastern Bluebird or Tree Swallow by occupying boxes or ejecting native residents. Primary vocalization is a monotonous chirping, which belies the presence of House Sparrow flocks tucked into roosting areas.

Male is chestnut above with gray forehead and grayish chest with variable black bib, thicker in breeding plumage and flecked with gray in winter.

Females are large and chunky, patterned in shades of tan, brown, and gray. Broad tan stripe over eye, single white wing bar, and thick bill.

Cedar Waxwing

Bombycilla cedrorum

L 6" | **WS** 11"

The sleek plumage of Cedar Waxwings makes them a welcome presence in a variety of habitats all across the state. Though increasing as a winter resident, especially along the coast, Cedar Waxwings migrate in large flocks during the last of May and make their way to coniferous, deciduous, or mixed forests, as well as towns and suburbs or any other habitat where they may feast on berries or other small fruits. Winter numbers fluctuate with the availability of fruit, but is generally increasing as human-planted ornamentals provide sustenance, and is currently regular from Bangor and Mount Desert Island south along the coast. Are occasionally known to become drunk on overripe berries, to their peril. Vocalization is a characteristic trilled, incessant whistle given by flying and perched flocks.

Creamy brown above with yellowish bellow, black face mask, brown crest, yellow tail tips. Waxy red tips on flight feathers not present on all individuals. Flocks stick closely together both in flight and while feeding.

Bohemian Waxwing

Bombycilla garrulus

L 8" | **WS** 14"

Winter visitors to Maine, sometimes quite common during "irruption" years, in other years not present at all. Breeds in the far north but comes south in winter, moving nomadically in large flocks with an almost supernatural sense for finding fruit. Flocks show up unpredictably at stands of Mountain Ash, crab apple, juniper, and other plants with dried or available fruit, frequently eating all there is before moving on, never to be seen again. Major winter flights occur about every 2-3 years, though sometimes in consecutive years. Distinguished from similar-looking Cedar Waxwing by larger size, white and yellow markings on wings, and red undertail. Vocalization is a laser-gun trill, lower-pitched and more clearly trilling than Cedar Waxwing.

Large and gray overall, with black on face, brown crest, yellow tail tips, and white and yellow feathering on wings.

Lapland Longspur

Calcarius lapponicus

L 6" | **WS** 10"

Lapland Longspurs are uncommon visitors in spring and fall as they travel between tundra breeding grounds and wintering areas in the U.S. Found in open areas like plowed fields or beaches, often in the company of other open country birds like Horned Larks or Snow Buntings. Uncommon in March and April, when may be encountered in its rich breeding plumage, but slightly more regular between October and November, where it may be picked out of flocks in appropriate habitat along the southern coast, such as the Popham Beach area, Kettle Cove, Scarborough Marsh, or Biddeford Pool. Few birds linger past mid-December. Call is a whistles *tleew*, followed in flight by a dry rattle.

Nonbreeding plumage encountered most often in Maine. Overall sparrow-like, with yellow bill, black facial "frame" beginning at eye. Breeding plumage (inset) is a stunning black head with chestnut nape. Forages by walking low and inconspicuously through grass, often in small, mixed flocks.

Snow Bunting

Plectrophenax nivalis

L 6" | **WS** 12"

A beautiful species of the Arctic tundra which visits Maine in winter. Tight flocks of Snow Buntings may be found in open country habitats such as bare roadsides, beaches, stubble fields, and parking lots. The birds flee the encroaching Arctic winter and appear in Maine in October, seen most often outside of heavily forested parts of the state such as agricultural fields in Aroostook County and open ground in central and southern Maine. Flocks are nervous and constantly on the move, moving every few minutes to a new spot as a wave, with individuals leap-frogging each other, their black-and-white wings flashing. Flocks roost together on open ground, often burrowing into the snow for warmth. Calls include a descending chew, and rattled *didididi*.

Nonbreeding plumage is rusty orange on a chunky white and black bird. Wings flashy white with black tips in flight; Tail black in center with white outer feathers.

Ovenbird
Seiurus aurocapilla

L 5" | **WS** 9"

The Ovenbird is a charming warbler of deep forests, difficult to see as it walks among the leaf litter but easily recognized by its ringing song. Ovenbirds arrive in early May and make their way into deciduous and mixed forests throughout the state, where they build Dutch oven-shaped nests on the forest floor which give the species its name. Fall migration runs late August to early October. Ovenbirds look and act like miniature thrushes, brown bodied and streak-chested, they high-step and head-bob across the forest floor in search of invertebrates. Their loud song may be heard in almost any forest in early and mid-summer, an explosive grouping of two-syllable phrases that increase in volume: teacher *TEACH-er TEACHER*. Flight song, often heard at night over wooded areas, is a complex series of notes mixed with teacher phrases; calls include a *chip* and *tink*.

Olive-brown above, white below with dense streaking. Orange crown bordered by black stripes. White eye ring, pink legs.

Blue-winged Warbler

Vermivora cyanoptera

L 5" | **WS** 7"

The Blue-winged Warbler has slowly expanded its range into southern Maine since the first breeding pairs were found in York County in 1980, but is still an uncommon migrant and rare breeder. They arrive in early May to brushy fields, forest edges, and shrublands, often located when their buzzy call is heard from a prominent perch in a tree. Of the few known breeding locations in Maine, Kennebunk Plains and River Point Conservation Area in Falmouth are most reliable. Blue-winged Warblers become slightly more common in early fall, when individuals disperse after breeding is complete and may turn up at migration hotspots along the southern coast. Blue-winged Warblers should be scrutinized for signs of hybridization with the closely-related Golden-winged Warbler. Most common song is a two-part buzz: *beee-BZZZZ* (or, helpfully, blue-*WINNGGGEED*).

Bright yellow head and underparts, black stripe through eye. Wings blue-gray with white wing bars.

Louisiana Waterthrush

Parkesia motacilla

L 6" | **WS** 10"

A recent arrival to Maine, Louisiana Waterthrush were only confirmed breeding in the state in 1980. Since then they have become more common, nesting along fast flowing streams in southern Maine. Look for this songster along the edge of brooks and streaks with hemlock trees and shaded ravines, such as Vaughn Woods in Hallowell, along the Merriland River in Wells, and similar spots in York, Cumberland, and Oxford counties, though the species is slowly expanding its range in Maine. Very similar in appearance to more common Northern Waterthrush; Louisiana typically whiter and more sparsely streaked, with white eyebrow stripe thick behind eye, narrow in Northern. Song is two or three clear, slurred notes followed by a fast tumble of more musical notes; call note is a loud *spich*.

Brown above and streaked white below, usually with unstreaked throat. Bold, broad white eye stripe from bill to back of head. Found bobbing its tail as it walks near clear flowing streams.

Northern Waterthrush
Parkesia noveboracensis

L 5 " | **WS** 9 "

Northern Waterthrush are early migrants, arriving in late April or early May, on their way to dense thickets near bogs, wooded swamps, lakes, ponds, streams, and other water bodies across the state. The hunt for insects and small vertebrates along the water's edge, bobbing their bodies as they walk like a Solitary Sandpiper. Thought to be more common outside of southern Maine, reliable locations for breeding Northern Waterthrush include Baxter State Park and Katahdin Woods and Waters National Monument, the Orono Bog Walk, Unity Pond, the Hidden Valley Nature Center in Jefferson, Brownfield Bog WMA, and others. Song is a resounding series of clear, sweet notes, accelerating and falling in pitch and ending with *whew whew whew*; call note is a hard *spwik*.

Brown above with yellowish tint to underparts and fine streaks on throat and belly. Eye stripe thinner and yellower than Louisiana.

Black-and-white Warbler

Mniotilta varia

L 5" | **WS** 8"

The amiable Black-and-white Warbler is a common migrant
and summer breeder, where, unusually for a warbler, it forages
by hopping along tree trunks and branches like a nuthatch,
prying insects out from crevices in the bark. The first migrants
return in early April, announced by their high-pitched,
"squeaky bicycle wheel" song, and the species spreads out
to mature deciduous or mixed forests throughout the state.
Though seen in trees, Black-and-white Warblers actually nest
on the ground, building tiny cup-shaped nests in the leaf litter.
The species is common in fall migration, especially along the
coast, which stretches from late August to early October, for
a few individuals linger later into the summer. Song is a high,
thin, deliberate *WEE see WEE see*; note is a sharp *stip*.

Small, striped like a referee. Creeps long tree trunks and large
tree branches. Note black spotting under tail, useful for
identification from below.

Female is less prominently striped, with cleaner face and
chest.

Tennessee Warbler

Leiothlypis peregrina

L 5" | **WS** 8"

Tennessee Warblers breed in the deep spruce-fir forests of far
northwestern Maine, and are uncommon elsewhere in migration
in May and between late August and early October. A small,
stocky warbler, Tennessee Warblers are seen actively moving
through canopies gleaning insects off branches and leaves.
Breeding generally confined to more remote northern areas,
though possible as far south as the Rangeley area, Baxter State
Park, and Mount Desert Island. Seen in a variety of wooded or
weedy habitats during migration. The song is especially helpful
in spring migration when the tiny birds may be otherwise
overlooked in tree canopies; listen for the loud, incessant three-
parted, ringing *sip-sip-sip, tibit-tibit-tibit ti ti ti ti ti*.

Breeding plumage
male is blue-
headed and
green-bodied with
prominent white
line above eye.

Fall birds greenish
and subtle, with
undertail feathers
lighter than breast,
faint wing bars,
and remnants of
whitish eye stripe.

Orange-crowned Warbler

Leiothlypis celata

L 5" | **WS** 7"

Orange-crowned Warblers are a nondescript species that does not breed in Maine but may be found in migration, especially later in fall. Most often encountered at coastal migratory hotspots in October in November, where it feeds low to the ground at weedy thickets, or perhaps snacking on suet or peanut butter from a backyard bird feeder. Sightings are grouped along the coast south of Bangor, including on Monhegan Island, Portland's Eastern Promenade, Biddeford Pool, the Rachel Carson NWR, and similar spots. Namesake orange head feathers are rarely seen. Call is a simple, emphatic *chip*.

Smally and uniformly olive green on adults and more grayish on young birds. Thin dark eyeline, white eye arcs, and smudgy streaks on breast. Yellow-green undertail helpful to separate from Tennessee Warbler.

Nashville Warbler

Leiothlypis ruficapilla

L 4″ | **WS** 7″

The Nashville Warbler is a common migrant and breeder throughout the state, focusing on areas of secondary growth in northern Maine: regenerating clearcuts, overgrown fields, clearings, and bogs. Arrives in early May and may be found anywhere warblers concentrate, singing their two part songs and foraging acrobatically at the ends of branches like tiny lemons. Fall migration peaks in September though some individuals may linger in October or later, often found in weedy thicket habitats. Of the many reliable spots to find Nashville Warblers in summer, try the Orono Bog Walk, Baxter State Park and Katahdin Woods and Waters NM, Acadia National Park, and the Rangeley area. Song is a two-parted, ending in a trill: *see-bit, see-bit, see-bit tititititi.*

Tiny and active, blue head contrasts with olive back. Throat and underparts bright yellow in spring, duller in fall. White eyering, white underbelly separating yellow on belly and under tail.

Mourning Warbler

Geothlypis philadelphia

L 5" | **WS** 7"

The intriguing and retiring Mourning Warbler is one of the last migrant warblers to arrive in Maine, showing up at the end of May or the beginning of June on its way to nest in dense undergrowth in the northern boreal forest. Mourning Warblers prefer areas disturbed, regrowing areas impacted by fire, insects, or human activities, and their numbers have trended downward in Maine as forest management practices have changed, particularly Downeast. Still reliable in boreal hotspots, including the Rangeley area and Quill Hill in Dallas Plantation, as well as suitable habitat further north. Migrates south early, beginning in August, and is most commonly found on offshore islands or the southern coast. Song is a loud, ringing *cheery-cheery-chory* usually with a downward note at the end.

Breeding male show dark gray hood with black bib, yellow underparts and olive green back. A skulker, the species is difficult to see when not singing from a perch. Females and juveniles show much fainter hood and clear but broken eye ring.

Common Yellowthroat

Geothlypis trichas

L 5" | **WS** 7"

The Common Yellowthroat is one of the most common breeding warblers in Maine, a near-constant presence in tangled vegetation at the edges of wet areas like ponds or marshes. Males are easily recognized by their black bandit masks, females drabber but separated by combination of yellowish throat and plain brown body. Common Yellowthroats arrive in May and spread to all corners of the state, where they are active and curious denizens of low grass and understory. Fall migration peaks in September, though lingering individuals are not unheard of into December. Common Yellowthroats frequently announce their presence, with a rollicking song of *wichety, wichety, wichety*, and a call note of a flat, *wet tchep*.

Black mask above yellow throat, white line on head, brown body. Distinctive crouching posture, tail often cocked.

Female and immatures are brownish overall, with varied gray on face, and contrasting white throat up to base of bill.

Cape May Warbler

Setophaga tigrina

L 5" | **WS** 8"

Uncommon during migration in southern Maine, Cape May Warblers breed in mature coniferous forests of northern and Downeast Maine, the southern limit of their range. A late arrival, Cape May Warblers peak at migratory hotspots in late May on their way north. They are patchy breeders in Maine, and subject to population fluctuations in response to spruce budworm outbreaks, but are most reliable in the Rangeley area, Baxter State Park, Cobscook Bay SP, and northern Aroostook County. Small numbers seen in fall migration, peaking in September, especially on Monhegan Island and other coastal hotspots. Song is a very high pitched, lilting *see-see-see-see*; call note is a high *tick*, and a thin *sip* is given in flight.

Stunning spring male yellow with chestnut face patch, streaked breast, and white wing patch.

Drab fall juvenile birds show gray-green tint, streaked underparts, and pale facial crescent useful for ID.

Female birds show less yellow, except for around face and on rump.

American Redstart

Setophaga ruticilla

L 5" | **WS** 7"

American Redstarts are active and entertaining warblers which are among the most common breeding warblers in the state. The Halloween coloration of spring males is unlike any other species, and the tail-flashing, insect-startling behavior of all individuals makes them difficult to miss. American Redstarts arrive in May and spread across the state to breed in deciduous forests, foraging for and pursuing insects through the mid-canopy and at the ends of branches. Fall migration extends from late August through October, when this species can be common at any migration hotspot. Song is frustratingly variable, but based around a series of squeaky notes ending with a somewhat sneeze-like, emphasized ending: *see-see-see-SEE-o*, or also a series of sweet, upslurred notes: *seet seet seet seet*; note is a sweep *chip*.

Jet black adult male shows orange wing and tail patches.

Females and young males gray headed, with yellow on tail and wings. American Redstarts flash their tails to startle insects out of hiding.

Northern Parula

Setophaga americana

L 5" | **WS** 7"

One of our most common and vocal warblers, the Northern Parula is found as a migrant and a breeder throughout the state. The species arrives in May and is often abundant in migrant flocks at any hotspot. Northern Parulas make their way to conifer-dominated forests, more common outside of southern Maine, where they seek out a hanging lichen called old man's beard to make their nests. Fall migration begins in late August and peaks in September, when the species is typically among the most common at coastal hotspots like Sandy Point in Yarmouth, Monhegan Island, and elsewhere. Unlike many Maine birds, Northern Parula numbers have trended upwards over the past fifty years. Distinctive song is a rapid, buzzy, upward trill that ends abruptly, as if in a sneeze.

Male small, slate blue with tequila sunrise pattern on chest, white eye arcs and wing bars, and green triangle on back.

Females and immatures lack bold chest patterning, but retain yellow breast, blue color, and green on back.

Magnolia Warbler

Setophaga magnolia

L 5" | **WS** 7"

The common and beautiful Magnolia Warbler has no special
affinity for its namesake tree, and instead seeks out spruce,
hemlock, or fir stands, as well as mixed second-growth forests
throughout the state. Its bright colors and habit of flashing
the white patches on its tail while hunting insects through the
mid-story combine to make this species a fairly evident species
at migratory hotspots between late April and early June. Breeds
in all counties but most common in dense forests of the western
mountains, north, and Downeast. Common and widespread
in fall migration, peaking in September. Song is a fast-paced,
squeaky series with an emphatic ending: *weeta weeta weeta
WHEW* or *sweetie sweetie SWEETEST*; call is a nasal *bzeep*.

Male yellow breasted with inky
necklace dripping down breast,
white eyebrow, gray head, black
on back with white wing bar.

Other plumages show less black,
with gray head and yellow breast
divided by pale gray necklace.
Varied streaking on breast and
flanks.

Bay-breasted Warbler

Setophaga castanea

L 6″ | **WS** 9″

Bay-breasted Warblers are large, stocky warblers of spruce and spruce-fir forests in northern Maine. Uncommon during spring and fall migrations, where its sluggish feeding technique and challenging song (which may be mistaken for the more common Black-and-white Warbler or American Redstart) make it easy to overlook. Maine's Bay-breasted Warbler population has declined due to habitat loss and a lack of spruce budworm outbreaks, but the species may still be found near Baxter SP or Katahdin Woods and Waters NM, Moosehorn NWR, the Topsfield area, and Aroostook NWR. Song is a high-pitched, squeaky-wheel *teetse teetse teetse*.

Large and dark-headed, with deep red cap, breast, and sides. White patch behind head, dark back, white wing bars.

Females and fall birds easily confused with Blackpoll Warbler, but show unstreaked breast, buffy (not yellow) sides.

Blackburnian Warbler

Setophaga fusca

L 5" | **WS** 8"

The flame-throated Blackburnian Warbler is a common and widespread breeding bird in Maine in mature coniferous and mixed-deciduous woodlands. Though its high-pitched song and habitat of singing and foraging from high in the canopy make it easy to overlook, one glance at its orange throat is all that's required for an identification. Fairly common in appropriate habitat throughout the state, especially north of Portland, reliable breeding locations including Morse Mountain in Phippsburg, Camden Bills SP, Mount Desert Island, Sunkhaze Meadows NWR, Borestone Mountain Audubon Sanctuary, and many more. Song is a rising, accelerating series of rapid notes: *tsi tsi tsi tsi ti ti ti* seeeee, also a squeaky *teesa teesa teesa* given when rival males meet.

Breeding male shows an electric orange throat, black back with white wing patch and white below.

Female muted, but orange on head and throat still distinctive. Juveniles even duller, with wash yellow replacing orange.

Yellow Warbler

Setophaga petechia

L 5" | **WS** 7"

Yellow Warblers are common and widespread as a migrant and a breeder in Maine. They are found across the state in brushy habitats near water, including willow thickets, lake and stream borders, wet field edges, and coastal shrubs. The bird's sunny color, easy-to-remember song, and eye-level foraging make it a conspicuous arrival in late April and early May, though duller plumage presents more of a challenge in the fall. Though Yellow Warblers have declined in Maine over the past fifty years, they are still common in appropriate habitat in all counties. Song is a clear and oft-repeated *seet-seet-seet oh-seet*, recalled by many birders as *sweet sweet, I'm so sweet*! Other calls include a clear chip note and a short, trilled *tzip* given in flight.

Male is bright yellow with orange streaking on chest. Note large black eye on plain face. Females duller and lack orange streaks.

Young birds in fall much duller, but are wash yellow all over, including under tail, with conspicuous black eye.

Blackpoll Warbler

Setophaga striata

L 6" | **WS** 9"

The half-ounce Blackpoll Warbler is famous for undertaking
the longest overwater migration of any songbird: a nonstop,
1,800-mile journey over the Atlantic from the coast of Maine,
New England, and Atlantic Canada to northern South America
each fall. They fly overland in spring, often arriving seemingly
all at once over just a few days in late May. Maine is at the
southern edge of their breeding range, and they may be found
on coastal islands Downeast or in high-elevation spruce-fir
forests, such as on Saddleback Mountain, Big Moose Mountain, Mount Katahdin, and other peaks. Blackpoll Warblers are
common along coastal migration spots in fall as they prepare
for their long journey south, though fall plumage can be a challenge. Song is a high-pitched series of staccato notes, slowly
rising and falling in pitch.

Males head appears
half-black and half-white,
with white wing bars and
a black-and-white
striped body.

Fall immature, common in migration, streaked olive above, variably yellowish below with indistinct streaks, undertail coverts white, feet yellow.

Female streaky and greenish above, faint streaks on white below, white wing bars, bright legs and feet

Chestnut-sided Warbler

Setophaga pensylvanica

L 4" | **WS** 8"

Chestnut-sided Warblers are common in migration and as breeding species in early second-growth brushlands, forest openings, orchards, powerline cuts, and other disturbed areas throughout the state. Arrives in early May and may be seen foraging actively, usually with its tail cocked, along thin branches. A common migrant in fall, seen inland through September with stragglers found along the coast or on offshore islands into early October. Early spring song is an assertive *wi-tea wi-tea wi-tea wheew*, with the ending either rising and emphasised or drooping, often remembered as *pleased pleased pleased to MEETCHA!* Males also sing a secondary song, typically later in summer, a varied, sweet warble often likened to the song of the Yellow Warbler.

Striking male has yellow cap, maroon sides, black-and-white face, and streaked back.

Fall birds show lime green back, white eyering, plain face and underparts, yellow wash on wings and back, may show remnant chestnut on sides.

Black-throated Blue Warbler
Setophaga caerulescens

L 5 " | **WS** 7 "

A lovely songbird of shady forest understory, the Black-throated Blue Warbler is a common breeding in deciduous and mixed-species forest, more common outside of southern Maine. The species migrates through Maine in May and occupies a wide swath of the Maine forest. Maine supports nearly 20% of the entire breeding population of Black-throated Blue Warblers, more than any other state. Though they forage low in the understory and are therefore often easier to see than canopy-dwelling warblers, Black-throated Blue Warblers are often heard before they are seen. Their song is a lazy, buzzy, ascending *zray-zray-ZREEEE* or *beer-beer-BEEE*.

Male deep blue above. Black face and flanks contrast with bright white belly. White wing patch.

Female drab olive above, with small white "pocket square" on wing feathers, unique to this species.

Palm Warbler

Setophaga palmarum

L 5" | **WS** 8"

Palm Warblers are one of the earlier migrant warblers to arrive in Maine, showing up in mid-April from wintering grounds in the southern U.S. Spring birds are from the distinct "yellow" eastern subspecies, and are common in weedy or brushy fields, or along beaches, easily identified by their lemony breast, red cap, and habitat of constantly pumping their tail up and down. The nest throughout northern and central Maine at the edges of open bogs ringed with conifers and at the edges of blueberry barrens Downeast. Yellow eastern birds are replaced in fall by the brownish western form, which can be very numerous at coastal hotspots during their late migration in early October. Song is a loose, buzzy trill made of 4 — 16 notes, frequently sung. Call note is a hearty chip.

"Yellow" birds breed in Maine. Yellow throat and underparts, streaked with red, and red cap. Constantly pumps tail.

"Western" population in fall is grayish brown with faintly streaked underparts with dusky, brownish cap, rump and undertail coverts dull yellow.

Pine Warbler

Setophaga pinus

L 5" | **WS** 8"

Unlike Magnolia Warbler or Palm Warbler, who rarely have
anything to do with their namesake plants, Pine Warblers are
birds of pine forests. They are some of the earliest warblers to
arrive, and their sweet, rolling trill may be heard from pine
stands throughout southern and central Maine, and their range
is expanding northward. Fall migration is late, peaking in
October, while some individuals may overwinter, regularly seen
visiting backyard bird feeders to eat suet. Song is a varied trill,
easily confused with the song of the Chipping Sparrow and
Dark-eyed Junco, though often slower and more musical than
those species. Call note is a flat *chip*.

Relatively large, yellow
on the front half with
unstreaked throat, yellow
"spectacles," white wing
bars, and sturdy bill.
Almost exclusively found
in pine trees.

Female and juveniles
drab and brownish, with
brownish cheeks, white
wing bars, and white tail
corners visible in flight.

Yellow-rumped Warbler

Setophaga coronata

L 5" | **WS** 9"

The Yellow-rumped Warbler is one of the most abundant warblers in Maine, and one of the few that regularly over-winters. Yellow-rumps are among the first warblers to arrive in Maine, showing up between March and May in occasion-ally large, conspicuous waves of birds. They breed in open coniferous forests across the state, more commonly outside of southern and central Maine, but are not as abundant as breeders as they are in migration. Fall migration peaks in October, and their ability to eat fruit, unique among warblers, permits some individuals to remain along the coast through the winter, especially at Two Lights SP, Biddeford Pool, Bailey Island, and other southern hotspots. Song is a sweet, weak trill with the last few phrases lower and faded: *swee swee swee SWEE swew swew*; note is distinctive chep, like a drop of water.

The bright yellow "armpits" and rump of male are evident, variable black streaking on white chest, black and blue back, black face mask.

Brown in winter with remnant yellow under wings and on rump, white eye-arcs and blurry streaks on chest.

Prairie Warbler

Setophaga discolor

L 4″ | **WS** 7″

A small, brightly-colored warbler of pine barrens, shrubby fields, powerline cuts, and other open second-growth habitats. Range is gradually expanding northward, but currently only breeds along the southern coast of Maine up through about Bangor. Breeding locations change often due to natural growth, but reliable locations in summer include Kennebunk Plains, Bond Brook Recreation Area in Kennebec County, the Brunswick Sand Plain, Saco Heath, and others. Song is a rapidly ascending series of buzzy notes, imaginatively described as the sound of a flying saucer taking off; note is a flat *chip*.

Small yellow warbler with unique black facial pattern and black streaks on sides. Often red streaking on yellowish back.

Females and juveniles show muted yellow and brown plumage, with faded but distinct facial pattern.

Black-throated Green Warbler

Setophaga virens

L 5" | **WS** 8"

One of the most common and widespread breeding warblers
in Maine, the Black-throated Green Warbler may be found in
coniferous forests and conifer-dominated mixed woods across
the state. Spring arrivals peak in May, and the species is often
among the most abundant warblers are migratory hotspots in
both spring and fall, peaking in September. Breeds throughout
Maine, though especially prefers forests with abundant white
pines and hemlocks, the latter tree at increasing risk from
hemlock woolly adelgid. Preferring to stay high in the treetops, Black-throated Green Warblers are often heard rather
than seen, but are known as incessant songsters and have
been recorded singing more than 450 times in one hour. Two
versions of the song may be heard, the first a rapid, buzzy
zee-zee-zee-zee-zoo-zee, or, for the mnemonically inclined,
black-black-black-throated-green! The second song is a lazy
zoo-zee-zoo-zoo-zee.

Back is green, but the thick black throat and yellow
face are most evident ID marks. Active in the high
canopy.

Female has yellow face, black streaks on sides.

Canada Warbler

Cardellina canadensis

L 5" | **WS** 8"

Canada Warblers are beautiful but uncommon and declining warblers of deciduous undergrowth and forests with thick, brushy understory. Appears in Maine towards the very end of May and fans out across the state to mature forests, less commonly in southern Maine than further north. Reliable breeding locations include the Bangor City Forest and Orono Bog Walk, Baxter SP and Katahdin Woods and Waters NM, Saco Heath, Gull Crest in Cape Elizabeth, and Moosehorn NWR. Has suffered a more than 65% decline since the 1960s, perhaps greater in Maine, thought to be due to forest management practices and the loss of forested wetlands. Song begins with a quick chip note before tumbling into a jumble of sweet, warbling notes.

Large, blue-gray, with yellow front and bold, restrained black necklace, whitish eye ring. Female similar but lacks necklace.

Wilson's Warbler

Cardellina pusilla

L 4" | **WS** 6"

A small, active warbler found flitting through the understory. They arrive in Maine in May and are uncommon but regular at most migratory hotspots before making their way to northern Maine to breed in brushy thickets near water, often in willow or alder. Uncommon and somewhat elusive as a breeder, they may be found in appropriate habitat at Cutler Coast Public Reserve Land, Acadia NP, the Rangeley and Carrabassett Valley area, and the Muscovic Road in Aroostook County. Whether you call is a cap, a beanie, a beret, or a toupee, the black patch on the top of a Wilson's Warbler's head distinguishes it from the similar Yellow Warbler, Song is a simple series of sweet notes which rise in intensity before fading at the end.

Tiny yellow warbler with black patch on crown.

Female lacks black cap, but shows yellow eyebrow, and olive cap, forehead, and behind eye.

Eastern Towhee

Pipilo erythrophthalmus

L 8" | **WS** 10"

A large, skulking sparrow, the Eastern Towhee is a widespread and fairly common breeder in brushy habitats in southern and central Maine. The species has declined in Maine in the past fifty years in large part due to their preferred habitat of old farm fields growing up into forest. They may still reliably be found in brushy thickets, powerline cuts, and other disturbed areas, their presence typically announced with a loud, carrying *two-WEE* call. Migrants arrive in late April to early May and depart by October, though individuals lingering into the winter along that coast are not uncommon, when they may visit bird feeders. Kennebunk Plains has long been perhaps the most reliable breeding location in Maine, along with Laudholm Farm, Brunswick Sand Plain, and Beech Hill Preserve in Rockport. Memorable song is a slow, clear *DRINK-your-TEAAA*!

Large and black with chestnut flanks and a white belly. Maine birds typically have red, not white, eye.

Female brown instead of black.

American Tree Sparrow

Spizelloides arborea

L 6" | **WS** 10"

American Tree Sparrows spend their summers in the open tundra and spend their winters in Maine, searching for seeds along the edges of snow-covered fields. Flocks of these hearty winter visitors wander freely in appropriate habitats, and their numbers in the state fluctuate from winter to winter. They generally arrive in October in the open fields and brushy areas of southern and central Maine, especially along the coast. They may show up at backyard feeders, and are often found at Gilsland Farm Audubon Center, Biddeford Pool, Laudholm Farm, Sears Island, Scarborough Marsh, and other open areas.Song may be heard in late winter, and is a pleasant jumble of sweet notes, generally descending. Flocking American Tree Sparrows call to each other with musical *tweedle-eet, tweedle-eet*.

Gray fronted, with variable rust-coloring on sides, reddish cap and eyeline, and white wing bars. Large dark spot on breast is most evident field mark.

Chipping Sparrow
Spizella passerina

L 5" | **WS** 8"

A very common and widespread summer resident, Chipping Sparrows are most readily seen feeding on the ground in lawns, parks, and other open areas. It breeds throughout the state, but somewhat less commonly in the dense forests of northern and Downeast Maine, and is a common visitor to backyard bird feeders. One of our "trilling" birds, the song of the Chipping Sparrow is easily confused with that of the Pine Warbler, Dark-eyed Junco, and other species, but the ground-loving habits, red cap, and white eye line make them easy to pick out in summer. Chipping Sparrows arrive in late April and are slow to leave, often lingering into early November and increasingly appearing wintering along the immediate coast. Song is long, dry, and delivered on a single pitch, and the call is a sharp *chip*.

Adults dull in winter, white eye stripe becoming buffy, bill pinkish. Juveniles birds heavily streaked, with pink bill and line through eye. Adult in summer is small and thin, with red cap, bold white eye stripe, and black line through eye.

Field Sparrow

Spizella pusilla

L 6" | **WS** 8"

A bright sparrow of open, brushy fields, the Field Sparrow reaches the northern limit of its breeding habitat in southern and coastal Maine. Generally arriving in early May, the species may be found as far Downeast as blueberry barrens in Washington County but is more common along the southern coast, in hotspots such as Kennebunk Plains, Brunswick Sand Plain, Capt. William Fitzgerald Recreation and Conservation Area in Brunswick, and Bond Brook Recreation Area in Fairfield. Southbound migration is protracted, and individuals are known to overwinter, especially along the southern coast. Song is a memorable series of clear whistles which accelerate rapidly, often likened to the sound of a ping-ping ball being dropped on a table. Field Sparrows give a number of calls, including a thin *seep* and a flat *chip*.

Plain bellied, with variable rufous wash, pink bill, white eye ring, and rufous cap and line behind eye. Often sits in the open for long periods.

Vesper Sparrow

Pooecetes gramineus

L 6" | **WS** 10"

The crisp Vesper Sparrow is a bird of grasslands and open country, uncommon in Maine save for appropriate habitat Downeast. Easily confused with other stripe-fronted sparrows, the white outer tail feathers of the Vesper are the most helpful feature when the bird is flushed. It's stronghold in the state are blueberry barrens in Washington County, where the species may be found singing from prominent perches and spending time feeding on the ground, particular in fields near Deblois and Columbia. Other reliable locations include McFarland Hill Delta in Ellsworth, California Fields Wildlife Area in Hollis, Kennebunk Plains, and dry agricultural fiends in Aroostook County. Song is similar to Song Sparrow, begins with paired whistles followed by musical trills ending in a jumble of notes.

A large brown sparrow, with long tail with white outer tail feathers obvious in flight. White eye ring, crisp breast streaking, and rarely-visible chestnut patch on wings.

Savannah Sparrow

Passerculus sandwichensis

L 5" | **WS** 8"

Savannah Sparrows are common in grasslands, marshes, weedy fields, dunes, and agricultural fields throughout Maine. Typically found on the ground in small flocks eating seeds, Savannah Sparrows are flightier and more connected to open habitat than the similar-looking Song Sparrow. Arrives in April and most migrants have moved south by October, though some individuals ofterwinter in dune or coastal habitat in southern Maine. A frosty-colored subspecies of Savannah Sparrow called the "Ipswich" Savannah Sparrow, which nests only on Sable Island off the coast of Nova Scotia, migrates in small numbers down the Maine coast in fall, and often overwinters at Scarborough Beach or the Popham Beach area. Song has mechanical and insect qualities, beginning with an accelerating series of notes followed by a drawn out, *tseee, tsaaaay*; Call note is a thin, fast *tsip*.

Small, brownish, strongly streaked back, breast streaking crisper than Song Sparrow. Usually shows yellow over eye.

Ipswich Sparrow large and pale grayish, with thin streaking. Only found in sand dunes and salt marshes in fall and winter.

Grasshopper Sparrow
Ammodramus savannarum

L 5″ | **WS** 8″

Grasshopper Sparrows are listed as Endangered under the Maine Endangered Species Act, and are regular breeders are just a few locations in southern Maine. The grassland habitat needed by Grasshopper Sparrows is in short supply in Maine, but they are relatively common at Kennebunk Plains and California Fields Wildlife Preserve in Hollis. Grasshopper Sparrows are solitary and typically stay out of sight on the ground, except for when singing from exposed perches. Sing is insect-like, beginning with a series of ticks followed by a metallic buzz: *tick tick tick tzzzzzzzzz.*

Small and buffy, with large bill, flat head, black stripes on crown, and variable yellow above eye and on bend of wing.

Nelson's Sparrow

Ammospiza nelsoni

L 5" | **WS** 8"

Nelson's Sparrows are small, skulking sparrows found in salt marshes scattered along the Maine coast. They may be seen darting through salt marsh vegetation, either on the ground or clinging to vegetation, and when flushed fly low and weakly over the marsh before plopping down out of sight. Reliable locations in summer include Laudholm Farm, Scarborough Marsh, Spurwink Marsh, Wharton Point in Brunswick, the Popham Beach area, Weskeag Marsh, Bass Harbor Marsh at Acadia NP, and appropriate salt marsh habitat in Machias and Lubec. May also be found in brackish marshes some miles inland along the Penobscot, Pleasant, and other rivers. Song is an unusual, rasping hiss, the sound of a drop of water being dropped onto a hot skillet.

Wash orange on breast, face, and sides, with grayish back and gray breast streaks. Black mark behind eye and on crown.

Saltmarsh Sparrow

Ammospiza caudacutus

L 5˝ | **WS** 7˝

The Saltmarsh Sparrow reaches the northern limit of its range along Maine's mid-coast. The two species overlap where the Saltmarsh Sparrow occurs in Maine, and great care should be taken to separate these two, skulking species. Look for the distinct white throat, the clear dark breast streaks and the face brighter than the breast to help identify a Saltmarsh Sparrow, but beware that hybrids are very common and a certain identification may not be possible. Saltmarsh Sparrow reach the northern limit of their range around Weskeag Marsh in Thomaston, and may also be found at Reid SP, the Popham Beach area, Spurwink Marsh, Scarborough Marsh, and Laudholm. High tide is the best place to look for these marsh sparrows, as the rising water may force them up into view. Song is a nonmusical series of hisses and clicks.

Small, large-billed, flat-headed. Distinct breast streaking, unlike Nelson's. Weak flier, often seen along the ground.

Fox Sparrow

Passerella iliaca

L 7" | **WS** 10"

The large and beautiful Fox Sparrow is an uncommon migrant
and rare but expanding breeder in Maine. They move through
southern Maine between mid-March and early April, typically
seen feeding on the ground, including underneath feeders, with
flocks of other sparrows. Was unknown as a breeding bird in
Maine until 1983 when it was discovered in northern Aroostook County, but since then continued south and west through
Baxter State Park as far as Saddleback Mountain and the
Sugarloaf area, where may be encountered in high elevation or
young, regenerating spruce-fir forests. Fall migration begins in
mid-October and some birds may linger into November. Song is
a loud, slightly husky set of whistled notes; note is a deep *chip*.

Large red and gray
sparrow, with red streaking
on white breast meeting
to make a central spot.

Song Sparrow

Melospiza melodia

L 6″ | **WS** 9″

The Song Sparrow is perhaps the most common and familiar sparrow in Maine, breeding nearly everywhere in the state save for the deep boreal forest. Found in a variety of habitats, including urban parks and landscaping, suburban backyards, weedy edges near water, forest edges, and fields. Migrants appear in March and depart beginning in September, though overwintering birds are fairly common along the southern coast. Generally stays on the ground or in low branches, feeds on a wide variety of insects and seeds, which may be taken from backyard feeders. It's song is unmissable in summer, and begins with several clear, drawn-out introductory notes before quickening into a jumble of highly variable musical notes and trills. Notes include a husky *jimp* and a high-pitched *tik*.

Brown sparrow with thick, heavy streaking on breast meeting in a messy central spot. Note thick stripes dropping from bill, framing white throat.

Lincoln's Sparrow

Melospiza lincolnii

L 6" | **WS** 8"

John James Audubon named this species after Thomas Lincoln, a resident of Dennysville, Maine and Audubon's companion on a collecting trip to Labrador in 1833, making the Lincoln's Sparrow the only species named after a Mainer. A boreal breeder, Lincoln's Sparrows are found in bogs and heaths in Downeast Maine and the northern and northwestern woods. They arrive in mid-May and are inconspicuous, skulking sparrows but which may be seen singing from low vegetation at Big Heath on Mount Desert Island, Boot Head Preserve and Quoddy SP in Washington County, and Aroostook NWR, and other locations. Fairly common between late September and mid-October in flocks of other migrating sparrows, especially along the coast. Song a lovely gurgle of musical notes, slightly husky, with several pitch changes. Note is a bland *chip*.

Like Song Sparrow but crisper and cleaner. Buffy breast with fine streaks which stop abruptly before white belly. Head feathers often raised.

Gray and brown head, fine streaking on back and along sides.

Swamp Sparrow

Melospiza georgiana

L 5" | **WS** 7"

A common but skulking species, Swamp Sparrows, as their name suggests, are nearly always found in dense vegetation near water. The first impression is often how dark they are: gray and dark red with a smudgy breast. They arrive in April and May and breed in wet and marshy areas throughout Maine, often wading into shallow water and dunking its head in pursuit of aquatic insects, behavior unlike any other sparrow. Fall migration begins in September and the birds may be found with other sparrows in grassy habitats, sometimes away from water. Individuals may linger into or through the winter along the southern coast. Their song is a rich trill given on one pitch, slower than Pine Warbler or Chipping Sparrow; notes include an emphatic *chip*, and a *zeeet* note given in flight.

Dark chestnut on wings and cap, overall gray face and smudgy gray breast, white throat, dark bill. Commonly perches in open to sing. Occasionally shows indistinct spot in center of breast. Perches in open to sing in spring and summer.

White-throated Sparrow

Zonotrichia albicollis

L 7" | **WS** 9"

Famous for its song, the White-throated Sparrow is a common breeding bird across the state and sometimes abundant in migration. They prefer nesting in coniferous or mixed wood forests, especially those with lots of shrubby understory, like regenerating timber stands. They arrive in Maine in late April and May and depart mostly in October, sometimes seemingly appearing in a wave overnight to swarm on the ground beneath a bird feeder or dominate the understory. Not uncommon in winter along the cost, typically at birdfeeders, and occasional winters see larger numbers. Occurs in two distinct head patterns, one striped in black and white and the other in tan and brown. Song is a clear, evocative *sooooo seeee dididi dididi dididi*, often remembered as "*Oh, Sam Peabody Peabody Peabody.*" Calls include a high, metallic *tink* and a high, level, *seeet* given in flight.

Plumage brightness varies between individuals, from bright to drab.

Large and large-headed, with bright white throat and black-and-white head stripes and yellow spot behind bill. Presence often announced by distinctive song.

White-crowned Sparrow

Zonotrichia leucophrys

L 6" | **WS** 9"

The bulky White-crowned Sparrow migrates through Maine on its way to and from breeding grounds in the high Arctic. It is uncommon but widespread when it arrives in spring, generally late April or early May, usually found in flocks of White-throated or other sparrows. Fall migration peaks in October, similarly uncommon and widespread, but more numerous in some autumns than others. Look for them with other sparrows in weedy areas, brush dumps, and other areas of brushy tangles, as well as under backyard bird feeders. Rare in winter, but possible along the southern coast. Song is a slow, whistled ramble of notes uncommonly heard in migration; call note a distinctive, sharp *pink*.

Immature, seen in fall, is large with pinkish bill, plain underparts, and rusty crown.

Adult is large and gray with bold black-and-white striping on head, and pink bill. Often on the ground or perched in shrubs.

Dark-eyed Junco

Junco hyemalis

L 6" | **WS** 9"

Dark-eyed Juncos are distinctive and charming sparrows found
nesting throughout Maine and increasing as a winter resident. They arrive early, in March, and are easily recognized by
their slate gray backs, snow white bellies, and white outer tail
feathers, obvious in flight. They are less common breeders in
southern Maine, though annual at Mt. Agamenticus, and prefer
coniferous forests, where they nest directly on the ground.
Common in winter in central and southern Maine, particularly at feeders. In winter and during migration they are most
commonly seen feeding on the ground in small flocks, flying
to the cover of low tree branches when disturbed. Five distinct
subspecies are recognized, with the "Slate-colored" form by far
the most numerous in Maine but others, including the black-
headed "Oregon" form, very rare but possible. Song is a steady,
musical trill lasting about two seconds, somewhat drier than
the similar Chipping Sparrow or Pine Warbler; notes are a
rapid twittering when feeding or flying.

Slate gray above and white
below, with pink bill. Females and
immatures more brownish than
males, especially on sides. White
outer tail feathers flash in flight
on all forms.

Scarlet Tanager

Piranga olivacea

L 7" | **WS** 11"

Scarlet Tanagers are an eye-popping summer resident of
mature deciduous forests throughout the state. They arrive in
May and are regular but not numerous migrants, and depart
in mid to late September. Those hungry for a look at a male in
breeding plumage may be frustrated by the species' skulking
treetop habits, which often make them difficult to locate. Most
common in central and southern Maine, regular summer locations for Scarlet Tanager include Kennebunk Plains, the Hidden
Valley Nature Center in Jefferson, Sieur de Monts Spring and Wild
Gardens in Acadia NP, and many other areas. Song is a hoarse
series of continuous phrases, sounding to many like a robin with a
sore throat. Distinctive call note is a hard *CHICK-brrr*.

Breeding plumage male
is an electric red, with
jet black wings and tail.

Females and
nonbreeding males are
yellow-green with dusky
wings and tail.

Northern Cardinal

Cardinalis cardinalis

L 9" | **WS** 11"

Though ubiquitous in southern and central Maine, the Northern Cardinal is still fairly uncommon in northern Maine. Only a confirmed breeder in the state since 1969, Northern Cardinals are continuing to expand northward as permanent residents in shrubby areas including backyards, parks, and forest edges. Pairs of Northern Cardinals form strong bonds, and the bright red male and the brown, red-billed female are never far apart in summer and in winter, though larger flocks often form in the fall. Suburban backyard habitats are the most reliable place to see Northern Cardinals, which readily eat from backyard feeders and are often the last species to visit at dusk and dawn. Sound is a very loud series of cheer notes followed by a laser-gun like ending of *chew-chew-chew* notes. Distinctive call is a hard, loud, metallic *tink*.

Male is red with red crest and bill, black face mask reaching to eye.

Female grayish brown with bright red-orange bill, reddish on crown and wings. Juvenile similarly structured but dark-billed lacking red.

Rose-breasted Grosbeak

Pheucticus ludovicianus

L 8"   **WS** 12"

The exuberantly-plumaged male Rose-breasted Grosbeak is found in mature deciduous forests throughout Maine and in early May migration, they often visit bird feeders.Breeding birds prefer regenerating deciduous forests and the edges of ponds, streams, and parks. Though brightly colored, Rose-breasted Grosbeaks can be tough to spot among the foliage, and are instead often located by song, similar to the American Robin but sweeter. River Point Conservation Area in Falmouth, Laudholm Farm, Sieur de Monts Spring and Wild Gardens at Acadia NP, and Katahdin Woods and Waters NM are among the many reliable locations to seek Rose-breasted Grosbeaks in summer. Song is delivered by both sexes, a rich, hurried jumble of warbled notes; note is a sharp *eenk* call, which sounds like a sneaker on a gym floor.

Black, red, and white plumage of breeding male is distinctive. Chunky and large-headed with white bill.

Females and nonbreeding males brown with massive pale bill, white breast with brown streaks, and boldly-striped head.

Indigo Bunting

Passerina cyanea

L 5" | **WS** 8"

The vibrant Indigo Bunting is commonly found in brusy, open habitat in southern and central Maine, including powerline cuts, brushy roadsides, overgrown fields, and field edges. They arrive in May and are fairly common along the coast to Ellsworth and north to Bangor, becoming scarce and local to the east and north. They may be seen in summer singing from powerlines or bush-tops at Essex Woods in Bangor, the Capt. William Fitzgerald Recreation and Conservation Area in Brunswick, Kennebunk Plains, California Fields Wildlife Area in Hollis, and other open, brushy locations. Fall migration begins in late August and lasts through October, when their decidedly less-glamorous plumage may cause identification challenges. Note small size, rich cinnamon-sugar brown color, and conical bill to help separate from sparrows. Song is a series of sweet notes, typically coupled: *sweet sweet, chew chew, seet seet* etc. repeated frequently throughout the day; notes include a sharp *chip*.

Breeding plumage male is entirely blue, bright and shining. Young or molting males often splotchy blue and brown.

Females and winter males in winter small and plain brown, overall warm brown, with hints of blue in wings and tail.

Rusty Blackbird

Euphagus carolinus

L 9" | **WS** 14"

A lovely, small blackbird of boreal bogs, the Rusty Blackbird is uncommon, and increasingly so, in northwestern Maine. In spring and fall it is glossy black with a contrasting pale eye, and is inconspicuous during its April migration. Its breeding range in Maine has contracted to less than half what it was in the early 1980s, part of a range-wide population crash of 85-99 percent in recent decades, due to habitat loss and other factors. Few reliable breeding locations, but they remain in bogs, beaver ponds and wet woods in boreal forest from the Rangeley area up through remote northwestern Maine. Fall migration runs between September and early November, when the species may be seen in its namesake orange plumage, often in flocks of other blackbirds, feeding in wet fields or near ponds. Song is a short series of squeaky notes ending higher, *koo-ah-koo-LEE*, sounding, aptly, like a rusty hinge; note is a soft *chuck*.

Male is somewhat glossy black with contrasting pale eyes. Females are gray-brown.

Immatures and winter adults have rusty feathering on back and head, with brighter eye stripe and contrasting dark eye patch.

Common Grackle

Quiscalus quiscula

L 12" | **WS** 16"

A harbinger of spring, Common Grackles arrive noisily as early as late February and find their way to suburban neighborhoods and open wetlands across Maine. They often travel in large, conspicuous flocks, easily identified as they fly overhead by their long tails and constant metallic creaking. The frequently nest colonially in stands of conifer, especially white pines, and feed in lawns, beneath backyard bird feeders, agricultural fields, parks, meadows, and marshes. Fall migration peaks in October, when flocks of Common Grackles thousands-strong may be seen moving south. Increasing as a winter visitor along the southern coast. Song is a series of squeaky, creaking notes, lethargic and unmusical; note is a low, loud *chack* usually given in flight.

A large, elongated blackbird with a long tail, purplish-blue iridescence on head and neck, and somewhat angry countenance. Long tail is often keel-shaped. Often travels in large, noisy flocks.

Red-winged Blackbird

Agelaius phoeniceus

L 9" | **WS** 14"

The Red-winged Blackbird is a gregarious and easily-identified resident of wet, marsh habitats, from the few cattails growing in a roadside ditch to extensive wetland complexes. One of the earliest migrants in spring, male Red-winged Blackbirds arrive as early as February to claim prime territories and await the brown-striped females. They are common breeders throughout the state, found nearly always near wetlands but not uncommon at backyard bird feeders, lawns, agricultural fields, and other places blackbirds gather. Red-winged Blackbirds often for massive flocks in fall as they head south, with individuals commonly lingering into December. Song is a distinctive *konk-a-REE*; note is a straightforward check, also a deep *click,* and drawn-out, descending whistle, and other sounds.

Male all black with bright red shoulder patches bordered with yellowish bar below. Bill sharply pointed.

Female and young heavily streaked with brown, like a large sparrow, with pointed bill and buffy eye-line.

Brown-headed Cowbird

Molothrus ater

L 7" | **WS** 12"

A small, nondescript blackbird, often found in mixed flocks of grackles, starlings, and other ground-feeding birds. The species arrives in late March and April, and work their way to open fields, pastures, suburban areas, and parks, where they mate and begin to look for nests. Not their own nests, however: Brown-headed Cowbirds are the most prolific "brood parasites" in Maine, and have been recorded laying their eggs in the nests of more than 140 other bird species, from Red-winged Blackbird to Ovenbird to Yellow Warbler. Cowbird eggs generally hatch first, and the nestlings are known to push the host's eggs out of the nest to command more attention. It's an unsettling but successful strategy, thought to have evolved as the birds followed mobile bison herds on the Great Plains. Song is an unusual liquid gurgle, ending with a high rusty note; also a series of high, clear, whistles.

Male with brown head, glossy black body. Often seen walking and feeding on lawns with raised tail.

Female uniform medium gray. Sharp, dark bill. Juveniles similar but lighter, may be seen being fed by another species

Bobolink
Dolichonyx oryzivorus

L 7" | **WS** 11"

A unique and charismatic blackbird, the Bobolink is a species of tall grass meadows and grasslands, habitats that have been rapidly disappearing from the state. They arrive in the first week of May and males begin performing elaborate aerial displays, fluttering into the air over the field and singing their incredible song before gliding back into the grass. Bobolink's preferred habitat has been declining in Maine and around the country due to regeneration of agricultural fields into forest, incompatible hay farming practices, and development, and the species is estimated to have lost more than 65% of its population in the past 50 years. However they are still common in appropriate habitat in southern and central Maine, and Aroostook County, at hotspots such as Gilsland Farm Audubon Center, Laudholm Farm, Wharton Point in Brunswick, and Weskeag Marsh. Song is an exuberant burst of metallic, bubbling notes, tinkles, and buzzes; note is a nasal *ink*, often given by migrants at night.

Breeding male has a black body with white up the back and on wings and a creamy yellow patch on the back of the head.

Female and nonbreeding male yellowish overall, like a large sparrow, with pinkish bill, head stripes, and clean nape.

Eastern Meadowlark

Sturnella magna

L 9" | **WS** 15"

A beloved resident of grasslands and hayfields, Maine's population of Eastern Meadowlark has declined as those habitats have been reduced, regenerated, or developed, and is now a Species of Special Concern in Maine. It breeds in suitable habitat along the coast, more common in the south, and still reliable at spots such as Kennebunk Plains, the Brunswick Sand Plain, and California Fields Wildlife Area. Spring arrivals may be found as early as March and the birds depart in September, though a few individuals may linger into winter in salt marshes. Song is a series of 3 to 5 clear whistled notes, such as *see-eee-ooh-say-ado*; note is a sputtering chatter.

Large, chunky, and short-tailed with flat head and long beak. Brownish with yellow throat and breast and black chest patch. White outer tail feathers obvious in flight.

Baltimore Oriole

Icterus galbula

L 7" | **WS** 11"

The brilliantly-colored Baltimore Oriole is a common breeding species in southern Maine and up through Aroostook County, with fewer birds found in boreal areas Downeast and in the northwest. Migration peaks in May, when Baltimore Orioles may be encountered singing from treetops or lured to backyard feeders by the presentation of an orange cut in half. They prefer nesting in open deciduous woodlands, such as found in open parkland with large stands or suburban neighborhoods, where their intricate hanging nests may be seen among the foliage. Fall migration peaks in September, when the species may be numerous at coastal migration hotspots, especially Monhegan Island. Song is a rich set of varied, piped whistles, often with long pauses between phrases. Notes include a dry chatter piping whistle, often with long pauses between phrases; notes include a varied chatter.

Breeding male bright orange with black head and back, and white wing bars.

Baltimore Orioles mostly eat insects and fruit, and occasionally drink nectar out of hummingbird feeders.

Female and immature male highly variable, from mostly orange to mostly gray. Underparts typically gray. Long, pointy, silver bill.

Orchard Oriole

Icterus spurius

L 7" | **WS** 10"

Smaller, darker, and more restricted in Maine than its Baltimore cousin, the Orchard Oriole is typically only found in York
and Cumberland Counties. They prefer areas of open woodland and scattered trees, often near water. Increasing in Maine
since the 1970s, Orchard Orioles are slowly expanding into
central Maine, but are still mostly found in the south, as spots
including Capisic Park in Portland, River Point Conservation
Area in Falmouth, the Timber Point Trail at Rachel Carson
NWR, and Gilsland Farm Audubon Center. Orchard Orioles
arrive in May and migrate south as early as the end of July.
Song is a rapid warbler, reminiscent of an American Robin but
squeakier, and often interspersed with chatters.

Breeding male is a deep
chestnut brown. Smaller
and thinner than Baltimore
Oriole.

Female lemon-yellow with
grayish back and white
wing bars. Young male
similar but with black
throat and face.

Common Redpoll

Acanthis flammea

L 5" | **WS** 8"

A small, lovely finch of the far north which irregularly visits Maine in winter. One of a handful of "winter finches" which irrupt southward in sometimes great abundance when preferred food crops in northern Canada are inadequate, Common Redpolls typically arrive in October and depart in April. During irruption years they may be found in a variety of habitats, but most reliable seem to be backyard bird feeders offering the nyjer seed preferred by small finches. Other potential habitats include open fields, beach edges, and suburban habitats where they seek birch or alder seeds. Their nomadic winter habit make them difficult to locate reliably, but listen for their dry, zapping notes in flight, similar to White-winged Crossbill, and a variety of goldfinch-like sounds.

Small whitish finch, with red cap, back and sides streaked with brown, and white wing bars. Male has pinkish wash on breast.

Female and young browner, more heavily streaked, and lack pink on breast.

Pine Siskin
Spinus pinus

L 5" | **WS** 8"

Pine Siskins are small and tidy finches with an irregular abundance, moving nomadically across the state in search of pine seeds. They are regular breeders in coniferous and mixed forests of eastern and northern Maine, but may breed anywhere, often early in spring before returning north after winter irruptions. Reliable locations for Pine Siskins in summer include the Nesowadnehunk Campground in Baxter SP; Mount Desert Island, and the Rangeley area but they may appear anywhere in winter, sometimes in large flocks at backyard bird feeders, but also deciduous forests, weedy fields, and anywhere else they may be able to procure seeds. Song is a disjointed ramble of chattering notes and rattled, punctuated with distinctive upslurred *zhreeeee* notes; flight note is a high-pitched *see-u*.

Small brown finch with brown streaked chest, pointy bill, and yellow on wings and sides of tail.

American Goldfinch

Spinus tristis

L 5" | **WS** 8"

One of Maine's most widespread and familiar residents, the American Goldfinch is easily attracted to backyard bird feeders offering nyjer and black oil sunflower seeds, but may also be found in weedy fields prying the seeds out of asters and thistles. Though a year-round resident, summer birds may move south in winter, to be replaced by birds from further north. The changing of the seasons is also highlighted by a dramatic molt, where the gleaming yellow males change into a drab brownish olive costume, a shift so complete that it's forgivable to think that an entirely different species is visiting the feeder. American Goldfinches typically nest later than other species, often beginning in August, to raise their young on an abundance of late-season seeds. Song is a cheery jumble of complex, high-pitched notes, punctuated periodically by a distinctive *cha-ree-ee-ee*; In flight American Goldfinches give a rich *po-tato chip po-tato chip* that, once learned, may be heard practically everywhere as flocks move overhead.

Summer male is bright yellow with black wings, black forehead, and white rump seen in flight.

Females and nonbreeding males grayish with variable yellow on head and wings. Often quite drab, but black-and-white wings distinctive.

Pine Grosbeak

Pinicola enucleator

L 9" | **WS** 14.5"

The robust Pine Grosbeak is a rare breeder in the boreal forests of the north and northwest and an irregular and irruptive visitor to other parts of Maine in winter. They nest in coniferous forests and subalpine habitat, confirmed from just a handful of locations in Maine but suspected in several more. They are more common in winter, though their presence varies greatly from year to year depending, mostly, on preferred seed crops further north. In irruptive years they may be fairly common but unreliable, as flocks move nomadically among the seeds of mountain ash, maple, and other woodland trees, as well as crabapples and berries on ornamental trees in developed areas. May also visit backyard bird feeders. In flight gives a quick, three-note whistle, *qui-di-leep*.

Male red and gray with white wing bars. Flocks feed quietly in trees and are easy to overlook.

Females have greenish-yellow patches on head, rump, and back. Large finch with stubby bill, white wing bars, and dark tail.

Evening Grosbeak
Coccothraustes vespertinus

L 8" | **WS** 14.5"

Evening Grosbeaks are large, lovely finches that irregularly breed
in northern Maine and are irruptive winter visitors into the rest
of the state in winter. Historically a western species, Evening
Grosbeaks expanded their range in the late 19th century in part
due to cyclical outbreaks of Spruce Budworm. Their numbers
peaked in Maine between the 1960s and 1990s, and have declined
ever since. Still they breed in spruce-fir forests, more commonly in
the far north, and undergo irregular winter irruptions southward,
where they may be found at backyard feeders. Though males may
be set to resemble a sunset, the name Evening Grosbeak was given
by early naturalists who mistakenly believed that the birds sang
mostly, or only, at night. Often first encountered by call note as the
bird flies overhead, Evening Grosbeaks emit a simple, descending
deewww note, or a burry rattle.

Male gorgeously patterned in yellow,
white, black, and brown, with large
grayish bill.

Females and juveniles grayish overall
with black and white wings, often some
yellow wash on collar or flanks.

Purple Finch
Haemorhous purpureus

L 6" | **WS** 10"

The richly-colored Purple Finch is the rural cousin of the
cosmopolitan House Finch. The species is a year round resident
in coniferous forests across Maine, though more numerous in
less-populated areas. Purple Finch populations irrupt southward every couple of winters and are sometimes quite common
at bird feeders in southern Maine, and sometimes into the
southeastern U.S. Competition with an expanding population
of House Finches is thought to contribute to a more than 50%
decline in Purple Finch numbers across their range, though the
species can still be quite common in appropriate habitat, as is
found at Baxter SP and Katahdin Woods and Waters NM; Essex
Woods in Bangor; Mount Desert Island; Kennebunk Plains;
Laudholm Farm; and elsewhere. Song is a slightly hoarse,
rambling warble; note is a sweet, whistled *tweedeelee*, and a
rich *tick* given in flight.

Small overall but large-headed. Male is rich
raspberry purple through back, rump, wings,
and sides—much more extensive coloring
than similar male House Finch.

Female brown and white, with thick
brown stripes on chest and bold brown
and white head striping, distinguishing
from bland female House FInch.

House Finch

Haemorhous mexicanus

L 6" | **WS** 9"

The House Finch is a common permanent resident in southern and eastern Maine, its range slowly expanding north. House Finches were unknown in the state before the early 1970s. Native to the American southwest, House Finches were illegally brought to New York City in the 1940s and sold as "Hollywood Finches," but released into the wild when the jig was up. Those birds began an incredible colonization of the East Coast and rest of the U.S. House Finches excel near human habitation, and are year-round visitors at bird feeders and often nest on or near buildings. Often confused with the similar Purple Finch, which, in males, show more color and lack brown streaking than House Finches and, for females, show a bolder head pattern. Song is a loud, rich, warble usually ending in a burry note with upward inflection. Call note is a soft, rising meowing note.

Brownish, streaked, and sparrow-sized, males show orange on the head, chest, and rump. Brown streaking on breast and sides, unlike Purple Finch.

Female brown with plain face. Grayish brown streaking below, sometimes quite blurry and indistinct.

Red Crossbill

Loxia curvirostra

L 6" | **WS** 11"

Fascinating members of the finch family, crossbills have evolved specialized bills to help them pry open the cones of conifer trees. Maine has two crossbill species, separated by a simple plumage difference and vocal details: the Red Crossbill and White-winged Crossbill. Both species are nomadic and irruptive, sometimes traveling far and wide in search of bumper crops of spruce, pine, hemlock, and other conifers. Nesting is similarly opportunistic: when feeding is good Red Crossbills may take advantage of the bounty and nest in any season. Red Crossbills may appear throughout the state, but typically breed in the coniferous forests of Downeast Maine, the western mountains and the north, and are regular at Baxter SP and Katahdin Woods and Waters NM, the Rangeley area, the Topsfield area, and Mount Desert Island. Presence often detected by flight call notes, a loud, repeated *gyp-gyp-gyp-gyp*. Song a series of short rattles, shrill whistles, and chip notes.

Adult males dull red with darker wings. Large crossed bill. Flocks often quiet and inconspicuous at treetop cones.

Female and young male varied yellowish to orange on body. Juveniles streaked brown like large Purple Finch.

White-winged Crossbill

Loxia leucoptera

L 6" **WS** 11"

Very similar in all respects to Red Crossbill, but with white
wing bars and different vocalizations. Found in coniferous
forests throughout Maine, more common in east, west, and
north, but highly nomadic. Distribution of crossbills in Maine
varies from year to year with changing cone crops. White-
winged Crossbills are uncommon but found in the same
habitats and hotspots, sometimes in larger flocks, as Red
Crossbills. Both crossbills more frequently appear outside of
their typically breeding areas in winter, when they may appear
in southern Maine or irrupt widely in search of good cone
crops. Flight call is a rapid *chit-chit chit-chit*, like a laser gun
battle, and song is a fast series of mechanical trills each set on a
different pitch.

Male red bodied, black wings with white
wing bars. Crossbills frequently visit
roadsides to eat sand and gravel to aid
digestion.

Females and young birds yellowish with
indistinct streaking.

Acknowledgments

I am filled with gratitude for the people in my life who set me on the course to writing this book and tolerated me during its production. First, my wonderful family, including my dad Will and grandfather Jon, for instilling a love for and fascination with nature; my mom Nancy, for her unyielding love and support; my brother Alex, for his humor and perspective; and, most importantly, my wife and son, Liz and Elliott, for their love and tolerance.

I'd like to thank Doug Hitchcox for his help reviewing this guide. Doug is for my money the best birder and most patient public naturalist this state will ever see. I'd also like to thank all the birders who've taught or adventured with me, including Jake Walker, Jason Hoeksema, Gene Knight, Ed Jenkins, Ian Carlsen, Mike Tucker, Jim Kravitz, the officers of DC Audubon, the Delta Wind Birds team, and many more.

I'd especially like to thank the good people at Destination St. John's (destinationstjohns.com), the Newfoundland-based group that brought me together with Nate Swick and Ted Floyd from the American Birding Association for a trip to the stunning Avalon Peninsula, where the seeds for this book were planted. After you're done exploring Maine, go up to St. John's and hire Jared Clarke. You'll love it.

Of course, a major thank you also goes to the American Birding Association (aba.org), an incredibly welcoming and joyful group. They do so much for our hobby. Please join their ranks.

Finally, thanks to George Scott at Scott & Nix, for his trust and assistance, and to Brian E. Small, for being such an incredibly gifted photographer.

Scott & Nix Acknowledgments

Many thanks to Jeffrey A. Gordon, Ted Floyd, John Lowry, Nathan Swick, and everyone at the American Birding Association for their good work. Thanks to Alan Poole, Miyoko Chu, and especially Kevin J. McGowan at the Cornell Lab of Ornithology for their bird measurement data sets. We give special thanks to Brian E. Small, and all the other contributors for their extraordinary photographs in the guide. We thank Chuck Hagner for his work on the manuscript; James Montalbano of Terminal Design for his typefaces; Charles Nix for the series design; and René Porter Nedelkoff and Nancy Wakeland of the Porter Print Group for help in shepherding this book through print production.

Image Credits

(T) = Top, (TR) = Top right, (B) – Bottom, (L) = Left, (R) = Right; pages with multiple images from one source are indicated by a single credit.

XII–XV Brian E. Small. XVI Joe Fuhrman. XX–XXXIII Brian E. Small. 2–43 Brian E. Small. 44–45 Mike Danzenbaker. 46 G. Malosh/VIREO. 47–48 Josh Gahagan. 49 Mike Danzenbaker. 50 Joe Fuhrman. 51 Rhinehard Geisler. 52–88 Brian E. Small. 89 Alan Murphy(T), Reinhard Geisler(B). 90–122 Brian E. Small. 123 Garth McElroy. 124–131 Brian E. Small. 132 Dennis Paulson(T), Allen T. Chartier(B). 133–138 Brian E. Small. 139 Garth McElroy. 140–142 Brian E. Small. 143 Joe Fuhrman(T), C. Murrant/VIREO(B). 144 Gregg Thompson. 145 Mike Danzenbaker. 146 S. Elowitz/VIREO(T), Joe Fuhrman (B). 147 G. Tepke/VIREO. 148–149 Joe Fuhrman. 150 Brian E. Small. 151 R. Curtis/VIREO(T), Brian E. Small(B). 152–154 Brian E. Small. 155 Jacob S. Spendelow. 156–165 Brian E. Small. 166 Brian E. Small, R. Curtis/VIREO(TR). 167–212 Brian E. Small. 213 Garth McElroy. 214–226 Brian E. Small. 227 Garth McElroy. 228–238 Brian E. Small. 239 Nick Lund(T), Brian E. Small(B). 240– 246 Brian E. Small. 247 Bob Steele(T), Brian E. Small(B). 248–294 Brian E. Small. 295 Alan Murphy.

Maine Bird Records Committee Checklist of Maine Birds

The Maine Bird Records Committee considers the following 465 species to be recorded with convincing evidence within the state of Maine. This list includes decisions made by the Committee through October 2020 and updated updated 1 June 2021. The names and taxonomic sequence follow the American Ornithologists' Union *Check-list* (7th edition, 1998) as amended by supplements (here through 61st supplement, July 2020).

Written descriptions and, if possible, photographs and/or audio or video should be submitted for any occurrence in the state. Please send all reports to the Secretary (bmarvil1@gmail.com).

Legend: * Rare † Extinct

**ANSERIFORMES
SWANS, GEESE & DUCKS–
ANATIDAE**
- ☐ *Black-bellied Whistling-Duck
- ☐ *Fulvous Whistling-Duck
- ☐ Snow Goose
- ☐ *Ross's Goose
- ☐ Greater White-fronted Goose
- ☐ *Pink-footed Goose
- ☐ Brant
- ☐ *Barnacle Goose
- ☐ Cackling Goose
- ☐ Canada Goose
- ☐ Mute Swan
- ☐ *Trumpeter Swan
- ☐ *Tundra Swan
- ☐ Wood Duck
- ☐ *Garganey
- ☐ Blue-winged Teal
- ☐ Northern Shoveler
- ☐ Gadwall
- ☐ Eurasian Wigeon
- ☐ American Wigeon
- ☐ Mallard
- ☐ American Black Duck
- ☐ Northern Pintail
- ☐ Green-winged Teal
- ☐ Canvasback
- ☐ Redhead
- ☐ Ring-necked Duck
- ☐ *Tufted Duck
- ☐ Greater Scaup
- ☐ Lesser Scaup
- ☐ *Steller's Eider
- ☐ King Eider
- ☐ Common Eider
- ☐ Harlequin Duck
- ☐ Surf Scoter
- ☐ White-winged Scoter
- ☐ Black Scoter
- ☐ Long-tailed Duck
- ☐ Bufflehead
- ☐ Common Goldeneye
- ☐ Barrow's Goldeneye
- ☐ Hooded Merganser
- ☐ Common Merganser
- ☐ Red-breasted Merganser
- ☐ Ruddy Duck

**GALLIFORMES
PHEASANTS, GROUSE &
TURKEY—PHASIANIDAE**
- ☐ Wild Turkey
- ☐ Ruffed Grouse
- ☐ Spruce Grouse
- ☐ *Willow Ptarmigan
- ☐ Ring-necked Pheasant

**PODICIPEDIFORMES
GREBES—
PODICIPEDIDAE**
- ☐ Pied-billed Grebe
- ☐ Horned Grebe
- ☐ Red-necked Grebe
- ☐ *Eared Grebe
- ☐ *Western Grebe
- ☐ *Clark's Grebe

**COLUMBIFORMES
PIGEONS & DOVES—
COLUMBIDAE**
- ☐ Rock Pigeon
- ☐ *Band-tailed Pigeon
- ☐ *Eurasian Collared-Dove
- ☐ † Passenger Pigeon
- ☐ White-winged Dove
- ☐ Mourning Dove

CUCULIFORMES
CUCKOOS—CUCULIDAE

☐ Yellow-billed Cuckoo
☐ Black-billed Cuckoo

CAPRIMULGIFORMES
NIGHTJARS—
CAPRIMULGIDAE

☐ Common Nighthawk
☐ *Chuck-will's-widow
☐ Eastern Whip-poor-will

APODIFORMES
SWIFTS—APODIDAE

☐ Chimney Swift

HUMMINGBIRDS—
TROCHILIDAE

☐ *Mexican Violetear
☐ Ruby-throated Hummingbird
☐ *Calliope Hummingbird
☐ *Rufous Hummingbird

GRUIFORMES
RAILS, GALLINULES &
COOTS—RALLIDAE

☐ *Clapper Rail
☐ *King Rail
☐ Virginia Rail
☐ *Corn Crake
☐ Sora
☐ Common Gallinule
☐ American Coot
☐ Purple Gallinule
☐ *Yellow Rail

CRANES—GRUIDAE

☐ Sandhill Crane

CHARADRIIFORMES
STILTS & AVOCETS—
RECURVIROSTRIDAE

☐ *Black-necked Stilt
☐ American Avocet

OYSTERCATCHERS—
HAEMATOPODIDAE

☐ American Oystercatcher

PLOVERS—
CHARADRIIDAE

☐ *Northern Lapwing
☐ Black-bellied Plover

☐ *European Golden-Plover
☐ American Golden-Plover
☐ *Pacific Golden-Plover
☐ Killdeer
☐ *Common Ringed Plover
☐ Semipalmated Plover
☐ Piping Plover
☐ *Wilson's Plover
☐ *Snowy Plover

SANDPIPERS—
SCOLOPACIDAE

☐ Upland Sandpiper
☐ Whimbrel
☐ † Eskimo Curlew
☐ *Long-billed Curlew
☐ *Bar-tailed Godwit
☐ Hudsonian Godwit
☐ Marbled Godwit
☐ Ruddy Turnstone
☐ *Great Knot
☐ Red Knot
☐ *Surfbird
☐ *Ruff
☐ Stilt Sandpiper
☐ *Curlew Sandpiper
☐ *Red-necked Stint
☐ Sanderling
☐ Dunlin
☐ Purple Sandpiper
☐ Baird's Sandpiper
☐ Least Sandpiper
☐ White-rumped Sandpiper
☐ Buff-breasted Sandpiper
☐ Pectoral Sandpiper
☐ Semipalmated Sandpiper
☐ Western Sandpiper
☐ Short-billed Dowitcher
☐ Long-billed Dowitcher
☐ American Woodcock
☐ Wilson's Snipe
☐ Spotted Sandpiper
☐ Solitary Sandpiper
☐ *Gray-tailed Tattler
☐ Lesser Yellowlegs
☐ Willet
☐ Greater Yellowlegs
☐ Wilson's Phalarope
☐ Red-necked Phalarope
☐ Red Phalarope

SKUAS—
STERCORARIIDAE

☐ Great Skua
☐ South Polar Skua
☐ Pomarine Jaeger
☐ Parasitic Jaeger
☐ *Long-tailed Jaeger

AUKS, MURRES &
PUFFINS—ALCIDAE

☐ Dovekie
☐ Common Murre
☐ Thick-billed Murre
☐ Razorbill
☐ † Great Auk
☐ Black Guillemot
☐ *Ancient Murrelet
☐ Atlantic Puffin
☐ *Tufted Puffin

GULLS, TERNS &
SKIMMERS—LARIDAE

☐ Black-legged Kittiwake
☐ *Ivory Gull
☐ Sabine's Gull
☐ Bonaparte's Gull
☐ Black-headed Gull
☐ Little Gull
☐ Laughing Gull
☐ *Franklin's Gull
☐ *Mew Gull
☐ Ring-billed Gull
☐ Herring Gull
☐ Iceland Gull
☐ Lesser Black-backed Gull
☐ *Slaty-backed Gull
☐ Glaucous Gull
☐ Great Black-backed Gull
☐ *Sooty Tern
☐ *Bridled Tern
☐ Least Tern
☐ *Gull-billed Tern
☐ Caspian Tern
☐ Black Tern
☐ *White-winged Tern
☐ Roseate Tern
☐ Common Tern
☐ Arctic Tern
☐ Forster's Tern
☐ Royal Tern
☐ *Sandwich Tern
☐ Black Skimmer

**PHAETHONTIFORMES
TROPICBIRDS—
PHAETHONTIDAE**

- [ ] *White-tailed Tropicbird
- [ ] *Red-billed Tropicbird

**GAVIIFORMES
LOONS—GAVIIDAE**

- [ ] Red-throated Loon
- [ ] *Pacific Loon
- [ ] Common Loon
- [ ] *Yellow-billed Loon

**PROCELLARIIFORMES
ALBATROSSES—
DIOMEDEIDAE**

- [ ] *Yellow-nosed Albatross
- [ ] *Black-browed Albatross

**AUSTRAL STORM-
PETRELS—OCEANITIDAE**

- [ ] Wilson's Storm-Petrel

**STORM-PETRELS—
HYDROBATIDAE**

- [ ] Leach's Storm-Petrel

**SHEARWATERS—
PROCELLARIIDAE**

- [ ] Northern Fulmar
- [ ] *Trindade Petrel
- [ ] *White-chinned Petrel
- [ ] Cory's Shearwater
- [ ] Sooty Shearwater
- [ ] Great Shearwater
- [ ] Manx Shearwater

**CICONIIFORMES
STORKS—CICONIIDAE**

- [ ] *Wood Stork

**SULIFORMES
FRIGATEBIRDS—
FREGATIDAE**

- [ ] *Lesser Frigatebird
- [ ] *Magnificent Frigatebird

**GANNETS & BOOBIES—
SULIDAE**

- [ ] *Masked Booby
- [ ] *Brown Booby
- [ ] Northern Gannet

**CORMORANTS—
PHALACROCORACIDAE**

- [ ] Great Cormorant
- [ ] Double-crested Cormorant

**PELECANIFORMES
PELICANS—
PELECANIDAE**

- [ ] American White Pelican
- [ ] *Brown Pelican

**BITTERNS & HERONS—
ARDEIDAE**

- [ ] American Bittern
- [ ] Least Bittern
- [ ] Great Blue Heron
- [ ] Great Egret
- [ ] *Little Egret
- [ ] *Western Reef-Heron
- [ ] Snowy Egret
- [ ] Little Blue Heron
- [ ] Tricolored Heron
- [ ] Cattle Egret
- [ ] Green Heron
- [ ] Black-crowned Night-Heron
- [ ] Yellow-crowned Night-Heron

**IBISES—
THRESKIORNITHIDAE**

- [ ] *White Ibis
- [ ] Glossy Ibis
- [ ] *White-faced Ibis
- [ ] *Roseate Spoonbill

**CATHARTIFORMES
NEW WORLD
VULTURES—
CATHARTIDAE**

- [ ] Black Vulture
- [ ] Turkey Vulture

ACCIPITRIFORMES

OSPREYS—PANDIONIDAE

- [ ] Osprey

**KITES, EAGLES &
HAWKS—ACCIPITRIDAE**

- [ ] *Swallow-tailed Kite
- [ ] Golden Eagle
- [ ] Northern Harrier

- [ ] Sharp-shinned Hawk
- [ ] Cooper's Hawk
- [ ] Northern Goshawk
- [ ] Bald Eagle
- [ ] *Mississippi Kite
- [ ] *Great Black Hawk
- [ ] Red-shouldered Hawk
- [ ] Broad-winged Hawk
- [ ] *Swainson's Hawk
- [ ] *Zone-tailed Hawk
- [ ] Red-tailed Hawk
- [ ] Rough-legged Hawk

**STRIGIFORMES
BARN OWLS—
TYTONIDAE**

- [ ] *Barn Owl

**TYPICAL OWLS—
STRIGIDAE**

- [ ] *Eastern Screech-Owl
- [ ] Great Horned Owl
- [ ] Snowy Owl
- [ ] Northern Hawk Owl
- [ ] *Burrowing Owl
- [ ] Barred Owl
- [ ] Great Gray Owl
- [ ] Long-eared Owl
- [ ] Short-eared Owl
- [ ] *Boreal Owl
- [ ] Northern Saw-whet Owl

**CORACIIFORMES
KINGFISHERS—
ALCEDINIDAE**

- [ ] Belted Kingfisher

**PICIFORMES
WOODPECKERS—
PICIDAE**

- [ ] Red-headed Woodpecker
- [ ] Red-bellied Woodpecker
- [ ] Yellow-bellied Sapsucker
- [ ] American Three-toed Woodpecker
- [ ] Black-backed Woodpecker
- [ ] Downy Woodpecker
- [ ] Hairy Woodpecker
- [ ] Northern Flicker
- [ ] Pileated Woodpecker

FALCONIFORMES
FALCONS—FALCONIDAE

- [ ] *Crested Caracara
- [ ] American Kestrel
- [ ] Merlin
- [ ] *Gyrfalcon
- [ ] Peregrine Falcon

PASSERIFORMES
TYRANT FLYCATCHERS—
TYRANNIDAE

- [ ] *Ash-throated Flycatcher
- [ ] Great Crested Flycatcher
- [ ] *Variegated Flycatcher
- [ ] *Tropical Kingbird
- [ ] Western Kingbird
- [ ] Eastern Kingbird
- [ ] *Gray Kingbird
- [ ] Scissor-tailed Flycatcher
- [ ] *Fork-tailed Flycatcher
- [ ] Olive-sided Flycatcher
- [ ] *Western Wood-Pewee
- [ ] Eastern Wood-Pewee
- [ ] Yellow-bellied Flycatcher
- [ ] *Acadian Flycatcher
- [ ] Alder Flycatcher
- [ ] Willow Flycatcher
- [ ] Least Flycatcher
- [ ] *Gray Flycatcher
- [ ] Eastern Phoebe
- [ ] *Say's Phoebe
- [ ] *Vermilion Flycatcher

SHRIKES—LANIIDAE

- [ ] *Loggerhead Shrike
- [ ] Northern Shrike

VIREOS—VIREONIDAE

- [ ] White-eyed Vireo
- [ ] *Bell's Vireo
- [ ] Yellow-throated Vireo
- [ ] *Cassin's Vireo
- [ ] Blue-headed Vireo
- [ ] *Plumbeous Vireo
- [ ] Philadelphia Vireo
- [ ] Warbling Vireo
- [ ] Red-eyed Vireo

JAYS & CROWS—
CORVIDAE

- [ ] Canada Jay

- [ ] Blue Jay
- [ ] American Crow
- [ ] Fish Crow
- [ ] Common Raven

LARKS—ALAUDIDAE

- [ ] Horned Lark

SWALLOWS—
HIRUNDINIDAE

- [ ] Bank Swallow
- [ ] Tree Swallow
- [ ] *Violet-green Swallow
- [ ] Northern Rough-winged Swallow
- [ ] Purple Martin
- [ ] Barn Swallow
- [ ] Cliff Swallow
- [ ] Cave Swallow

CHICKADEES &
TITMICE—PARIDAE

- [ ] Black-capped Chickadee
- [ ] Boreal Chickadee
- [ ] Tufted Titmouse

NUTHATCHES—SITTIDAE

- [ ] Red-breasted Nuthatch
- [ ] White-breasted Nuthatch

CREEPERS—CERTHIIDAE

- [ ] Brown Creeper

WRENS—
TROGLODYTIDAE

- [ ] *Rock Wren
- [ ] House Wren
- [ ] Winter Wren
- [ ] *Sedge Wren
- [ ] Marsh Wren
- [ ] Carolina Wren

GNATCATCHERS—
POLIOPTILIDAE

- [ ] Blue-gray Gnatcatcher

KINGLETS—REGULIDAE

- [ ] Golden-crowned Kinglet
- [ ] Ruby-crowned Kinglet

OLD WORLD
FLYCATCHERS—
MUSCICAPIDAE

- [ ] *Northern Wheatear

THRUSHES—TURDIDAE

- [ ] Eastern Bluebird
- [ ] *Mountain Bluebird
- [ ] Townsend's Solitaire
- [ ] Veery
- [ ] Gray-cheeked Thrush
- [ ] Bicknell's Thrush
- [ ] Swainson's Thrush
- [ ] Hermit Thrush
- [ ] Wood Thrush
- [ ] *Fieldfare
- [ ] *Redwing
- [ ] American Robin
- [ ] Varied Thrush

MOCKINGBIRDS &
THRASHERS—MIMIDAE

- [ ] Gray Catbird
- [ ] Brown Thrasher
- [ ] *Sage Thrasher
- [ ] Northern Mockingbird

STARLINGS—STURNIDAE

- [ ] European Starling

WAXWINGS—
BOMBYCILLIDAE

- [ ] Bohemian Waxwing
- [ ] Cedar Waxwing

OLD WORLD
SPARROWS—
PASSERIDAE

- [ ] House Sparrow

PIPITS—MOTACILLIDAE

- [ ] American Pipit

FRINGILLINE &
CARDUELINE FINCHES—
FRINGILLIDAE

- [ ] *Common Chaffinch
- [ ] Evening Grosbeak
- [ ] Pine Grosbeak
- [ ] *Gray-crowned Rosy-Finch
- [ ] House Finch

- ☐ Purple Finch
- ☐ Common Redpoll
- ☐ Hoary Redpoll
- ☐ Red Crossbill
- ☐ White-winged Crossbill
- ☐ *Eurasian Siskin
- ☐ Pine Siskin
- ☐ *Lesser Goldfinch
- ☐ American Goldfinch

LONGSPURS— CALCARIIDAE

- ☐ Lapland Longspur
- ☐ *Chestnut-collared Longspur
- ☐ *Smith's Longspur
- ☐ Snow Bunting

NEW WORLD SPARROWS— PASSERELLIDAE

- ☐ *Cassin's Sparrow
- ☐ Grasshopper Sparrow
- ☐ *Black-throated Sparrow
- ☐ Lark Sparrow
- ☐ *Lark Bunting
- ☐ Chipping Sparrow
- ☐ Clay-colored Sparrow
- ☐ Field Sparrow
- ☐ *Brewer's Sparrow
- ☐ Fox Sparrow
- ☐ American Tree Sparrow
- ☐ Dark-eyed Junco
- ☐ White-crowned Sparrow
- ☐ *Golden-crowned Sparrow
- ☐ *Harris's Sparrow
- ☐ White-throated Sparrow
- ☐ Vesper Sparrow
- ☐ *LeConte's Sparrow
- ☐ Seaside Sparrow
- ☐ Nelson's Sparrow
- ☐ Saltmarsh Sparrow
- ☐ *Henslow's Sparrow
- ☐ Savannah Sparrow
- ☐ Song Sparrow
- ☐ Lincoln's Sparrow
- ☐ Swamp Sparrow
- ☐ *Green-tailed Towhee
- ☐ Eastern Towhee

YELLOW-BREASTED CHATS—ICTERIIDAE

- ☐ Yellow-breasted Chat

BLACKBIRDS & ORIOLES—ICTERIDAE

- ☐ Yellow-headed Blackbird
- ☐ Bobolink
- ☐ Eastern Meadowlark
- ☐ *Western Meadowlark
- ☐ Orchard Oriole
- ☐ *Bullock's Oriole
- ☐ Baltimore Oriole
- ☐ Red-winged Blackbird
- ☐ *Shiny Cowbird
- ☐ *Bronzed Cowbird
- ☐ Brown-headed Cowbird
- ☐ Rusty Blackbird
- ☐ *Brewer's Blackbird
- ☐ Common Grackle

WOOD-WARBLERS— PARULIDAE

- ☐ Ovenbird
- ☐ Worm-eating Warbler
- ☐ Louisiana Waterthrush
- ☐ Northern Waterthrush
- ☐ *Golden-winged Warbler
- ☐ Blue-winged Warbler
- ☐ Black-and-white Warbler
- ☐ Prothonotary Warbler
- ☐ *Swainson's Warbler
- ☐ Tennessee Warbler
- ☐ Orange-crowned Warbler
- ☐ Nashville Warbler
- ☐ *Virginia's Warbler
- ☐ Connecticut Warbler
- ☐ *MacGillivray's Warbler
- ☐ Mourning Warbler
- ☐ *Kentucky Warbler
- ☐ Common Yellowthroat
- ☐ Hooded Warbler
- ☐ American Redstart
- ☐ *Kirtland's Warbler
- ☐ Cape May Warbler
- ☐ *Cerulean Warbler
- ☐ Northern Parula
- ☐ Magnolia Warbler
- ☐ Bay-breasted Warbler
- ☐ Blackburnian Warbler
- ☐ Yellow Warbler

- ☐ Chestnut-sided Warbler
- ☐ Blackpoll Warbler
- ☐ Black-throated Blue Warbler
- ☐ Palm Warbler
- ☐ Pine Warbler
- ☐ Yellow-rumped Warbler
- ☐ Yellow-throated Warbler
- ☐ Prairie Warbler
- ☐ *Black-throated Gray Warbler
- ☐ *Townsend's Warbler
- ☐ *Hermit Warbler
- ☐ Black-throated Green Warbler
- ☐ Canada Warbler
- ☐ Wilson's Warbler

GROSBEAKS & BUNTINGS— CARDINALIDAE

- ☐ Summer Tanager
- ☐ Scarlet Tanager
- ☐ Western Tanager
- ☐ Northern Cardinal
- ☐ Rose-breasted Grosbeak
- ☐ *Black-headed Grosbeak
- ☐ Blue Grosbeak
- ☐ *Lazuli Bunting
- ☐ Indigo Bunting
- ☐ Painted Bunting
- ☐ Dickcissel

Species Index

A

Acanthis flammea, 287
Accipiter
  cooperii, 69
  gentilis, 70
  striatus, 68
Actitis macularius, 107
Aegolius acadicus, 87
Agelaius phoeniceus, 280
Aix sponsa, 4
Alca torda, 146
Alle alle, 147
Ammodramus savannarum, 263
Ammospiza
  caudacutus, 265
  nelsoni, 264
Anas
  acuta, 12
  crecca, 13
  platyrhynchos, 10
  rubripes, 11
Anthus rubescens, 221
Antigone canadensis, 94
Antrostomus vociferus, 155
Archilochus colubris, 158
Ardea
  alba, 58
  herodias, 56
Ardenna
  gravis, 47
  grisea, 48
Arenaria interpres, 111
Asio flammeus, 85
Aythya
  affinis, 17
  collaris, 15
  marila, 16
  valisineria, 14

B

Baeolophus bicolor, 199
Bartramia longicauda, 108
Bittern, American, 55
Blackbird
  Red-winged, 280
  Rusty, 278
Bluebird, Eastern, 210
Bobolink, 282
Bombycilla
  cedrorum, 224
  garrulus, 225
Bonasa umbellus, 35
Botaurus lentiginosus, 55
Brant, 2
Branta
  bernicla, 2
  canadensis, 3
Bubo
  scandiacus, 84
  virginianus, 88
Bucephala
  albeola, 21
  clangula, 28
  islandica, 29
Bufflehead, 21
Bunting
  Indigo, 277
  Snow, 227
Buteo
  jamaicensis, 76
  lagopus, 78
  lineatus, 74
  platypterus, 75
Butorides virescens, 61

C

Calcarius lapponicus, 226

Calidris
  alba, 113
  alpina, 119
  bairdii, 117
  canutus, 120
  fuscicollis, 118
  maritima, 112
  melanotos, 116
  minutilla, 115
  pusilla, 114
Calonectris diomedea, 46
Canvasback, 14
Cardellina
  canadensis, 255
  pusilla, 256
Cardinalis cardinalis, 275
Cardinal, Northern, 275
Catbird, Gray, 218
Cathartes aura, 66
Catharus
  bicknelli, 213
  fuscescens, 212
  guttatus, 215
  ustulatus, 214
Cepphus grylle, 143
Certhia americana, 202
Chaetura pelagica, 156
Charadrius
  melodus, 102
  semipalmatus, 101
  vociferus, 100
Chickadee
  Black-capped, 196
  Boreal, 198
Childonias niger, 138
Chordeiles minor, 154
Chroicocephalus philadelphia, 127
Circus hudsonius, 71
Cistothorus palustris, 206
Clangula hyemalis, 26
Coccothraustes vespertinus, 291

Coccyzus
  americanus, 152
  erythropthalmus, 153
Colaptes auratus, 166
Columba livia, 150
Contopus
  cooperi, 168
  virens, 169
Coot, American, 93
Cormorant
  Double-crested, 52
  Great, 54
Corthylio calendula, 209
Corvus
  brachyrhynchos, 188
  corax, 186
  ossifragus, 189
Cowbird, Brown-headed, 281
Crane, Sandhill, 94
Creeper, Brown, 202
Crossbill
  Red, 294
  White-winged, 295
Crow
  American, 188
  Fish, 189
Cuckoo
  Black-billed, 153
  Yellow-billed, 152
Cyanocitta cristata, 185

D

Dolichonyx oryzivorus, 282
Dove, Mourning, 151
Dovekie, 147
Dowitcher, Short-billed, 121
Dryobates
  pubescens, 164
  villosus, 165
Dryocopus pileatus, 167
Duck
  American Black, 11
  Harlequin, 20
  Long-tailed, 26

Ring-necked, 15
Ruddy, 34
Wood, 4
Dumetella carolinensis, 218
Dunlin, 119

E

Eagle
Bald, 72
Egret
Great, 58
Snowy, 59
Egretta
caerulea, 60
thula, 59
Eider, Common, 18
Empidonax
alnorum, 172
flaviventris, 170
minimus, 171
traillii, 173
Eremophila alpestris, 183
Euphagus carolinus, 278

F

Falcipennis canadensis, 36
Falco
columbarius, 79
peregrinus, 82
sparverius, 80
Falcon, Peregrine, 82
Finch
House, 293
Purple, 292
Flicker, Northern, 166
Flycatcher
Alder, 172
Great Crested, 175
Least, 171
Olive-sided, 168
Willow, 173
Yellow-bellied, 170
Fratercula arctica, 148
Fulica americana, 93

Fulmar, Northern, 50
Fulmarus glacialis, 50

G

Gadwall, 8
Gallinago delicata, 122
Gallinula galeata, 92
Gallinule, Common, 92
Gannet, Northern, 51
Gavia immer, 38
Gavia stellata, 40
Geothlypis
philadelphia, 236
trichas, 237
Gnatcatcher, Blue-gray, 207
Goldeneye
Barrow's, 29
Common, 28
Goldfinch, American, 289
Goose, Canada, 3
Goshawk, Northern, 70
Grackle, Common, 279
Grebe
Horned, 42
Pied-billed, 41
Red-necked, 43
Grosbeak
Evening, 291
Pine, 290
Rose-breasted, 276
Grouse
Ruffed, 35
Spruce, 36
Guillemot, Black, 143
Gull
Bonaparte's, 127
Glaucous 133
Great Black-backed, 134
Herring, 130
Iceland, 132
Laughing, 128
Lesser Black-backed, 136
Ring-billed, 129

H

Haematopus palliatus, 96
Haemorhous
   mexicanus, 293
   purpureus, 292
Haliaeetus leucocephalus, 72
Harrier, Northern, 71
Hawk
   Broad-winged, 75
   Cooper's, 69
   Red-shouldered, 74
   Red-tailed, 76
   Rough-legged, 78
   Sharp-shinned, 68
Heron
   Black-crowned Night-, 62
   Great Blue, 56
   Green, 61
   Little Blue, 60
Hirundo rustica, 195
Histrionicus histrionicus, 20
Hummingbird, Ruby-throated, 158
Hydrobates monorhis, 45
Hylocichla mustelina, 216

I

Ibis, Glossy, 63
Icterus
   galbula, 284
   spurius, 286

J

Jaeger, Parasitic, 142
Jay
   Blue, 185
   Canada, 184
Junco, Dark-eyed, 273
Junco hyemalis, 273

K

Kestrel, American, 80
Killdeer, 100
Kingbird, Eastern, 176
Kingfisher, Belted, 157
Kinglet
   Golden-crowned, 208
   Ruby-crowned, 209
Kittiwake, Black-legged, 126
Knot, Red, 120

L

Lanius borealis, 177
Lark, Horned, 183
Larus
   argentatus, 130
   delawarensis, 129
   fuscus, 136
   glaucoides, 132
   hyperboreus, 133
   marinus, 134
Leiothlypis
   celata, 234
   peregrina, 233
   ruficapilla, 235
Leucophaeus atricilla, 128
Limnodromus griseus, 121
Longspur, Lapland, 226
Loon
   Common, 38
   Red-throated, 40
Lophodytes cucullatus, 30
Loxia
   curvirostra, 294
   leucoptera, 295

M

Mallard, 10
Mareca
   americana, 9
   strepera, 8
Martin, Purple, 190
Meadowlark, Eastern, 283

Megaceryle alcyon, 157
Melanerpes carolinus, 160
Melanitta
    americana, 22
    deglandi, 25
    perspicillata, 24
Meleagris gallopavo, 37
Melospiza
    georgiana, 269
    lincolnii, 268
    melodia, 267
Merganser
    Common, 32
    Hooded, 30
    Red-breasted, 33
Mergus
    merganser, 32
    serrator, 33
Merlin, 79
Mimus polyglottos, 220
Mniotilta varia, 232
Mockingbird, Northern, 220
Molothrus ater, 281
Morus bassanus, 51
Murre
    Common, 144
    Thick-billed, 145
Myiarchus crinitus, 175

N

Nannopterum auritus, 52
Nighthawk, Common, 154
Numenius phaeopus, 110
Nuthatch
    Red-breasted, 201
    White-breasted, 200
Nycticorax nycticorax, 62

O

Oceanites oceanicus, 44
Oriole
    Baltimore, 284
    Orchard, 286
Osprey, 64

Ovenbird, 228
Owl
    Barred, 86
    Great Horned, 88
    Northern Saw-whet, 87
    Short-eared, 85
    Snowy, 84
Oxyura jamaicensis, 34
Oystercatcher, American, 96

P

Pandion haliaetus, 64
Parkesia
    motacilla , 230
    noveboracensis, 231
Parula, Northern, 241
Passer domesticus, 223
Passerculus sandwichensis, 262
Passerella iliaca, 266
Passerina cyanea, 277
Perisoreus canadensis, 184
Petrel
    Leach's Storm-, 45
    Wilson's Storm-, 44
Petrochelidon pyrrhonota, 194
Pewee, Eastern Wood-, 169
Phalacrocorax carbo, 54
Phalarope
    Red-necked, 125
    Red, 124
Phalaropus
    fulicarius, 124
    lobatus, 125
Pheucticus ludovicianus, 276
Phoebe, Eastern, 174
Picoides
    arcticus, 163
    dorsalis, 162
Pigeon, Rock, 150
Pinicola enucleator, 290
Pintail, Northern, 12
Pipilo erythrophthalmus, 257
Pipit, American, 221
Piranga olivacea, 274

Plectrophenax nivalis, 227
Plegadis falcinellus, 63
Plover
  American Golden-, 97
  Black-bellied, 98
  Piping, 102
  Semipalmated, 101
Pluvialis
  dominica, 97
  squatarola, 98
Podiceps
  auritus, 42
  grisegena, 43
Podilymbus podiceps, 41
Poecile
  atricapillus, 196
  hudsonicus, 198
Polioptila caerulea, 207
Pooecetes gramineus, 261
Porzana carolina, 91
Progne subis, 190
Puffin, Atlantic, 148
Puffinus puffinus, 49

Q

Quiscalus quiscula, 279

R

Rail, Virginia, 90
Rallus limicola, 90
Raven, Common, 186
Razorbill, 146
Redpoll, Common, 287
Redstart, American, 240
Regulus satrapa, 208
Riparia riparia, 193
Rissa tridactyla, 126
Robin, American, 217

S

Sanderling, 113
Sandpiper
  Baird's, 117
  Least, 115

  Pectoral, 116
  Purple, 112
  Semipalmated, 114
  Solitary, 106
  Spotted, 107
  Upland, 108
  White-rumped, 118
Sapsucker, Yellow-bellied, 161
Sayornis phoebe, 174
Scaup
  Greater, 16
  Lesser, 17
Scolopax minor, 123
Scoter
  Black, 22
  Surf, 24
  White-winged, 25
Seiurus aurocapilla, 228
Setophaga
  americana, 241
  caerulescens, 249
  castanea, 243
  coronata, 252
  discolor, 253
  fusca, 244
  magnolia, 242
  palmarum, 250
  pensylvanica, 248
  petechia, 245
  pinus, 251
  ruticilla, 240
  striata, 246
  tigrina, 238
  virens , 254
Shearwater
  Cory's, 46
  Great, 47
  Manx, 49
  Sooty, 48
Shoveler, Northern, 7
Shrike, Northern, 177
Sialia sialis, 210
Siskin, Pine, 288

Sitta
    canadensis, 201
    carolinensis, 200
Snipe, Wilson's, 122
Somateria mollissima, 18
Sora, 91
Sparrow
    American Tree, 258
    Chipping, 259
    Field, 260
    Fox, 266
    Grasshopper, 263
    House, 223
    Lincoln's, 268
    Nelson's, 264
    Saltmarsh, 265
    Savannah, 262
    Song, 267
    Swamp, 269
    Vesper, 261
    White-crowned, 272
    White-throated, 270
Spatula
    clypeata, 7
    discors, 6
Sphyrapicus varius, 161
Spinus
    pinus, 288
    tristis, 289
Spizella
    passerina, 259
    pusilla, 260
Spizelloides arborea, 258
Starling, European, 222
Stelgidopteryx serripennis, 192
Stercorarius parasiticus, 142
Sterna
    dougallii, 139
    hirundo, 140
    paradisaea, 141
Sternula antillarum, 137
Strix varia, 86
Sturnella magna, 283

Sturnus vulgaris, 222
Swallow
    Bank, 193
    Barn, 195
    Cliff, 194
    Northern Rough-winged, 192
    Tree, 191
Swift, Chimney, 156

T

Tachycineta bicolor, 191
Tanager, Scarlet, 274
Teal
    Blue-winged, 6
    Green-winged, 13
Tern
    Arctic, 141
    Black, 138
    Common, 140
    Least, 137
    Roseate, 139
Thrasher, Brown, 219
Thrush
    Bicknell's, 213
    Hermit, 215
    Swainson's, 214
    Wood, 216
Thryothorus ludovicianus, 203
Titmouse, Tufted, 199
Towhee, Eastern, 257
Toxostoma rufum, 219
Tringa
    flavipes, 105
    melanoleuca, 104
    semipalmata, 109
    solitaria, 106
Troglodytes
    aedon, 204
    hiemalis, 205
Turdus migratorius, 217
Turkey, Wild, 37
Turnstone, Ruddy, 111
Tyrannus tyrannus, 176

U

Uria
   aalge, 144
   lomvia, 145

V

Veery, 212
Vermivora cyanoptera, 229
Vireo
   Blue-headed, 179
   Philadelphia, 181
   Red-eyed, 182
   Warbling, 180
   Yellow-throated, 178
Vireo
   flavifrons, 178
   gilvus, 180
   olivaceus, 182
   philadelphicus, 181
   solitarius, 179
Vulture, Turkey, 66

W

Warbler
   Bay-breasted, 243
   Black-and-white, 232
   Black-throated Blue, 249
   Black-throated Green, 254
   Blackburnian, 244
   Blackpoll, 246
   Blue-winged, 229
   Canada, 255
   Cape May, 238
   Chestnut-sided, 248
   Magnolia, 242
   Mourning, 236
   Nashville, 235
   Orange-crowned, 234
   Palm, 250
   Pine, 251
   Prairie, 253
   Tennessee, 233
   Wilson's, 256
   Yellow-rumped, 252
   Yellow, 245
Waterthrush
   Louisiana, 230
   Northern, 231
Waxwing
   Bohemian, 225
   Cedar, 224
Whimbrel, 110
Whip-poor-will, Eastern, 155
Wigeon, American, 9
Willet, 109
Woodcock, American, 123
Woodpecker
   American Three-toed, 162
   Black-backed, 163
   Downy, 164
   Hairy, 165
   Pileated, 167
   Red-bellied, 160
Wren
   Carolina, 203
   House, 204
   Marsh, 206
   Winter, 205

Y

Yellowlegs
   Greater, 104
   Lesser, 105
Yellowthroat, Common, 237

Z

Zenaida macroura, 151
Zonotrichia
   albicollis, 270
   leucophrys, 272

Nick Lund, a conservationist, author, and birder is the advocacy and outreach manager at Maine Audubon. He writes online under the name The Birdist (@TheBirdist), and his birding and nature writing has appeared in *Audubon* magazine, *Slate.com*, the *Washington Post*, the *Portland Phoenix, National Geographic.com, National Parks Magazine, the Maine Sportsman, Down East Magazine, Popular Science.com,* and others. He lives in Cumberland, Maine.

Brian E. Small is a full-time professional bird and nature photographer. For more than 30 years, he has traveled widely across North America to capture images of birds in their native habitats. He served as the photo editor for *Birding* magazine for 15 years. Small grew up in Los Angeles, graduated from U.C.L.A. in 1982, and still lives there today with his wife Ana, daughter Nicole, and son Tyler.

Quick Index

See the Species Index for a complete listing of all the birds in the *American Birding Association Field Guide to Birds of Maine.*

Bittern, 55
Blackbirds, 278–280
Bluebird, 210
Bobolink, 282
Brant, 2
Bufflehead, 21
Buntings, 227, 277
Canvasback, 14
Cardinal, 275
Catbird, 218
Chickadees, 196–198
Coot, 93
Cormorants, 52–54
Cowbird, 281
Crane, 94
Creeper, 202
Crossbills, 294–295
Crows, 188–189
Cuckoos, 152–153
Dove, 151
Dovekie, 147
Dowitcher, 121
Ducks, 4, 11, 15, 20, 26, 34
Dunlin, 119
Eagle, 72
Egrets, 58–59
Eider, 18
Falcon, 82
Finches, 292–293
Flicker, 166
Flycatchers, 168–175
Fulmar, 50
Gadwall, 8

Gallinule, 92
Gannet, 51
Gnatcatcher, 207
Goldeneyes, 28–29
Goldfinch, 289
Goose, 3
Goshawk, 70
Grackle, 279
Grebes, 41–43
Grosbeaks, 276, 290–291
Grouse, 35–36
Guillemot, 143
Gulls, 127–136
Harrier, 71
Hawks, 68–78
Herons, 56, 60–62
Hummingbird, 158
Ibis, 63
Jaeger, 142
Jays, 184–185
Junco, 273
Kestrel, 80
Killdeer, 100
Kingbird, 176
Kingfisher, 157
Kinglets, 208–209
Kittiwake, 126
Knot, 120
Lark, 183
Longspur, 226
Loons, 38–40
Mallard, 10
Martin, 190
Meadowlark, 283
Mergansers, 30–33
Merlin, 79
Mockingbird, 220

Murres, 144–145
Nighthawk, 154
Nuthatches, 200–201
Orioles, 284–286
    Baltimore, 284
Osprey, 64
Ovenbird, 228
Owls, 84–86
Oystercatcher, 96
Parula, 241
Petrels, 44–45
Pewee, 169
Phalaropes, 124–125
Phoebe, 174
Pigeon, 150
Pintail, 12
Pipit, 221
Plovers, 97–102
Puffin, 148
Rail, 90
Raven, 186
Razorbill, 146
Redpoll, 287
Redstart, 240
Robin, 217
Sanderling, 113
Sandpipers, 106–118
Sapsucker, 161
Scaup, 16–17
Scoters, 22–25
Shearwaters, 46–49
Shoveler, 7
Shrike, 177
Siskin, 288

Snipe, 122
Sora, 91
Sparrows, 223, 258–272
Starling, 222
Swallows, 191–19
Swift, 156
Tanager, 274
Teal, 6, 13
Terns, 137–141
Thrasher, 219
Thrushes, 213–21
Titmouse, 199
Towhee, 257
Turkey, 37
Turnstone, 111
Veery, 212
Vireos, 178–182
Vulture, 66
Warblers, 229–25
Waterthrush, 230–231
Waxwings, 224–225
Whimbrel, 110
Whip-poor-will, 155
Wigeon, 9
Willet, 109
Woodcock, 123
Woodpeckers, 160–167
Wrens, 203–206
Yellowlegs, 104–105
Yellowthroat, 23